Welcome to the Digital World...

Morgan Govereau

Thanks for Your
Help & involvement
With the HCOS forums
this Year.

Pastor Daniel Knorr

Are you ready?
Are your children ready?
Is your church ready?
Do you even know what the questions are?

Be sure to visit the companion website to this book at:

www.ChristianThinker.org

Each Chapter has its own webpage including every hyperlink used in the book. You will find additional quotes and a blog to start a dialog about our Digital World. You can subscribe to the Christian-Thinker.org newsletter and RSS-feed Podcast by Greg.

Additional copies can be ordered online and discounts may apply for special orders.

Discipling This Generation For A Digital World is available in audio, unabridged and read by the author.

The 4 CD Set can also be ordered at ChristianThinker.org for the same price as the book.

Discipling This Generation For A Digital World

Greg Bitgood

Forward By
David Kalamen

Published by:
ChristianThinker.org

Discipling This Generation for a Digital World

Copyright © 2006 by Gregory J. Bitgood

Published by ChristianThinker.org
   2260 Omineca Place,
   Kelowna, British Columbia, Canada, V1V 1H7
   www.ChristianThinker.org   info@ChristianThinker.org

Cover Design by Clint Schnee of Isotope 12
First Printing 2006
Printed by Source Graphics, Kelowna, BC, Canada

Library and Archives Canada Cataloguing in Publication
Bitgood, Greg, 1958-
       Discipling this generation for a digital world / Greg Bitgood; forward by David Kalamen.
Includes bibliographical references and index.
ISBN 0-9780762-0-6
1. Technology--Religious aspects--Christianity. 2. Christian life.
I. Title.
BR115.T42B48 2006   261.56   C2006-902139-2

Scripture taken from *The Message* by Eugene H. Peterson Copyright 1993, 1994, 1995, 1996, 2000, 2001, 2002. Used by permission of NavPress Publishing Group.

Scripture quotations marked (KJV) are *King James Version,* Authorized King James Version. Public Domain

Scripture taken from the HOLY BIBLE, NEW INTERNATIONAL VERSION®. Copyright © 1973, 1978, 1984 International Bible Society. Used by permission of Zondervan. All rights reserved.

The "NIV" and "New International Version" trademarks are registered in the United States Patent and Trademark Office by International Bible Society. Use of either trademark requires the permission of International Bible Society.

I dedicate this book to my great-grandchildren, Patrick Fuentes and Sally Bitgood, who will either be in cyber-university when they access the audible version of this book found in the Google archives, or in jail when a sadistic guard notices the last name of the author and throws a copy of the book that was found in the smoldering ruins of the Christian camps.

Table of Contents

Acknowledgements 10

Forward 12

Introduction.. 15
   Where are all the Prophets? 17
   This is not *Digital for Dummies* 19
   Is a Digital World Good or Bad?....................................... 20

Section One - Understanding the Concepts 25

What is so "Digital" about this World? 27
   The First Digital Electronic Communication 29
   Digital Communication Changes Everything................. 31
   The New Emerging Technology....................................... 32
   The Digital Switch 34
   Digital Ubiquity 35
   Moore's Law.. 38

Discipleship – The Biggest Word in Christianity 41
   God is a Green Light... 43
   Becoming All Things To All People 45
   Amish in the City 48
   Aliens in this World 50
   The Context of Discipleship.. 52
   The Curriculum of Discipleship 55
   The Means of Discipleship.. 58

Section Two - The Four Digital Transformations
.... **63**

The Communication Revolution........................ 65
  A Lesson from Socrates.. 65
  The Church's Earliest Gift of Technology...................... 67
  We All Want to Change the World............................ 69
  Moveable Type - The Catalyst for World Change 71
  The Reformation 73
  The Modern Gutenberg-ian Invention...................... 77
  The New Language of Communication...................... 82
  Communication Disciples 86
  Online Accountability 89
  Where is Martin Luther?..................................... 90

Globalization 94
  The First Worldwide Movement............................ 101
  Globalization 1.0, 2.0 and 3.0 104
  No More Borders 106
  Who is My Neighbor?... 109
  Global Government or Not 113
  Let's Not Forget our Christian Mandate 115

Informationalism... 118
  And Then There Was Google................................ 120
  Just Google It 125
  Google Is Watching You...................................... 127
  Google Morality... 129
  Knowledge Puffs Up.. 131

Biotechnology.. 136
  Biology + Digital World = Biotechnology.................. 138
  Mapping the Human Genome 142
  Enhancing the Species.. 144
  The Stem Cell Debate.. 150
  Hello Dolly.. 153
  This is Greg and my other Clone Greg 155
  Belle – the Telekinetic Monkey............................. 158
  More Human or More Machine 160

Section Three - The Digital Future **165**

The Doubling 167
   Exponential "Doubling" or Back to Moore's Law.......... 169
   Nanotechnology – Smaller is Bigger 173
   Computer Doubling will Double Almost Everything ... 175
   The Digital World in 2016 176
     Communication in 2016...177
     Globalization in 2016..179
     Informationalism in 2016......................................181
     Biotechnology in 2016 182
   Conclusion of the Matter 184

Epilogue: A Tale of Two Futures............................... 187
   2056 – The Enhanced Future......................................188
   2056 – The Deprived Future...................................... 196
   Postscript to These Stories 202

Index 205

Acknowledgements

I tend to be a last minute guy. This means that I have to put a team of people around me to cover my hind parts. If you were covering and I missed you, please forgive me; at my age the view back there can be a bit obscure.

Christine is the love of my life; she also has the distinction of being my first wife. Without her, there is no book and probably I am not much to look at either. She was my main proofreader and editor. She endured my lively defense with any change to this book. You're my friend for life.

My four kids: Richard (and his soon to be married wife, Chelsea), Christabelle, Josiah and Kenny all had to put up with my constant rants on how good this story was and how amazing that technology is. Thanks for putting up with me.

Pastor Dave Kalamen has been my friend and inspiration. He did not give me much sympathy as a bit of pay back for when he was writing his last book. Thank you for the honorable things said in the Forward; I hope to live up to them.

My editing team worked right up to the day this was printed. My mom, Betty did the most work. Thanks for looking after your boy, mom. Also kudos to Clint at Isotope 12 (who also designed the cover). Gord and Joanne Robideau, Dave McGrew, Ted Gerk, Suzanne Johnson and Chris McGrath all gave me great feedback. Thanks guys.

I also am very grateful to my staff at the Schools and the Church. Michi, Suzanne, Teresa, Kathy, Barb and Alicia all tried their best to keep the phone calls to a minimum. My admin teams were helpful in covering for me: Steve and Steve, Chris, Janet, Ted, Sarah, Brodie, Dan, Trudy, Jeremy. I have the privilege of working with some of the best disciplers in the world.

Thank you MTI class of 2005/06 who were my guinea pigs while I was writing discipleship. Thank you HCS and HCOS grade 11 & 12 classes for giving me lots to write about.

Special thanks to Marion McKeown, owner of Twenty-Seven Soldiers Publishing Company who gave me some very helpful advice. Thanks to Candis at the Prior House Inn for her hospitality when a part of this book was written and finally Rob at Source Graphics, Kelowna who got this to the press and out in time for my launch date (or so I hope).

Forward

Just a few months prior to this book's publication, I asked Greg for the privilege of writing the forward to what I believe is going to be the first of many books and articles on this subject. He honored me with this opportunity.

My reasoning was two-fold. Firstly, I have always had a passion to see Christianity move into cultural relevance without moral or biblical compromise, and the title and topic intrigued me. But, secondly, I felt that you needed to know what I know about the author, the man behind the message.

I have been Greg's pastor, fellow elder, and friend for more than two decades. We have 'grown older together,' fought some cultural battles together, prayed, worshiped and wept together, planned and envisioned together. There have been few men who have so passionately pursued the call as Greg has. He has given himself - his life, his broad skill set, his finances, his time and energy - to God and His cause. His family reflects those same values.

The first time I met Greg and Christine it was abundantly clear that their passion for reaching the next generation was deeply embedded into their hearts. For years, they faithfully served by ministering Sunday after Sunday to the children of Kelowna Christian Center. Within time, their stewardship of these lives was enlarged to include the youth ministry, then on to the administration of Heritage Christian School and Preschool, the oversight of our Ministry Training Institute, and now, it has resulted in the conception and birthing of the highly influential Heritage Christian Online School.

They have been unwavering in faith and faithfulness. The scripture states that when a man is found faithful in that which belongs to another (another man's responsibility or vision), God gives them that which can be considered their own (Lu 16:12). I have been delighted to see their development into educational leaders and visionaries for this emerging generation: they have sown honorably, and they are now reaping an apostolic vision of their own.

Greg has always had a love for the word of God, and in his prayer times has often recited the apostolic prayers. A common, fundamental element to every one of these prayers has been the request that a spirit of wisdom and revelation rest upon the Church (Eph 1:17; Col 1:9). I sincerely believe that God has granted Greg his prayer, and released to him revelation as to the times and seasons the Church is in, and wisdom as to how to conduct itself in difficult timoo.

This book is a prophetic word into the future of the post-modern Church. It is a call to the Church to know God, but also to engage His Holy Spirit so as to locate the ways to use technologies and methodologies available to them to reach their own generation. It is a call to embrace culture without yielding to its spirit, to be a counter-culture movement that takes the lead, becoming the head and not the tail, history makers.

My son, Brodie stated in one of his messages recently, "One generation's ceiling is the next generation's platform." Well, Greg has raised the ceiling with this book. He has placed a challenge to those of us blessed to be alive on this side of the year 2,000. He has requested intelligent interaction with culture, informed faith within the Church, discernment of the times we are living in, and a revelatory response to the challenges the message we are bringing to society is experiencing. How are you going to respond?

This is not an easy read, but it is an important read. I pray that you will be able to enter Greg's mind and hear his heart. And, I sincerely pray that you are able to go beyond the history and theology and touch destiny with the message of this book.

David Kalamen
Kelowna BC, Canada
April 5th, 2006

Rev. David Kalamen is Senior Pastor of Kelowna Christian Center (www.kcc.net). He has served in this role since April 1982. His apostolic leadership has made this church one of the leading voices in Canada and the world for the gospel. He has been recognized nationally for his work in the Pro-Life Movement in Canada. He serves as a national director in the ministerial fellowship of O.B.F.F. His ministry has taken him to five continents and he has recently published "Life Purpose" which can be ordered online at:
www.kcc.net/lifepurpose/index.htm

Introduction

The dogmas of the quiet past are inadequate to the stormy present. The occasion is piled high with difficulty, and we must rise with the occasion. As our case is new, so we must think anew and act anew.

Abraham Lincoln[1]

The thin dirt road stretched out before us appearing and disappearing along the narrow ridges of the northern Mexican desert. The ten of us were traveling in a rented van behind the big red Ford truck of Barbara and Calvin Scott, missionaries that I have been working with for many years. We lunged up and down these narrow ridges into dried out gullies that would become impassable if we were caught in a storm during the rainy season. We had turned south from Cananea, a mining town about 20 kilometers from the Arizona-Sonora border and were on our way to the pueblo of Bacanuchi.

It was the spring of 2005 but the coolness of the season burned off quickly in the morning. The thermometer was reaching 85 degrees Fahrenheit or rather 29 degrees

---

[1] ed. Roy P. Basler, *The Collected Works of Abraham Lincoln,* vol. V, Rutgers University Press, New Brunswick, N. J., 1953, p. 537. President ABRAHAM LINCOLN's annual message to Congress, December 1, 1862. This passage was quoted in the preamble to the 1968 Republican party platform

Celsius for the nine Canadians on board (I still think in Fahrenheit). We had been told that this community had never had an evangelical witness with the exception of a Christmas program held there five months earlier. We were going into a community that had not been evangelized before and yet it was only about three hours south of the US-Mexican border.

The eight Canadian students and one teacher were all from Heritage Christian Online School. These students were all from different parts of British Columbia and came to our Christian school every day via the internet. We had only met the students in person the week before and here we were ready to dramatize the gospel message in a village two thousand miles from home.

We were in remote Sonora. The houses were mostly made from adobe thatch bricks with the exception of a few concrete brick buildings. The people were a darker mixture of native Indian-Latin decent. The older villagers still wore some of the traditional native clothing while the younger villagers and children had a more western look with clothing from the racks of Wal-Mart across the border.

Our presentation, given outside in the town square across from the local school, went very well for the two hundred or so locals who attended. Many responded, in the closing moments of the presentation, and prayed to receive Christ as their Savior. Most of the villagers would consider themselves good Catholics but the priest only made it into town every three to six months. They hungered for a deeper understanding of Jesus and the gospel.

After the presentation we lingered for some time visiting with our new friends. I joined a conversation or rather an attempt at conversing between three of our Canadian girls and three girls of similar age from Bacanuchi. Our broken Spanish made communication somewhat challenging but we were able to convey our ideas. I attempted to communicate that these students all went to school over the internet via their computers every day. The three girls just nodded. It was obvious to me that I wasn't communicating very well because they just nodded and smiled. Whenever I tell someone back home that we have hundreds of students participating every day in Christian education via the internet, I receive many "oohs" and "ahs," but these three were unimpressed. I attempted again to convey the idea that these students went to school over the internet. *Did the girls even know what the internet was?* I wondered. Again, they smiled and nodded.

After another failed attempt for a response, they looked at me in an odd way; the way someone looks when they wonder if you really know what you are talking about. They pointed to their one room school building, painted green and probably the fanciest structure in town, and there on the opposite corner was a small satellite dish. They explained that they too go to school via the internet. Every day they attend classes at the high school in Cananea via their remote satellite connection over the internet. They had been using this technology for the last two years and were happy that we have the same opportunity in Canada.

We are in a Digital World and everything has changed, from the little schoolroom in the Sonoran desert to the huge metropolises around the world.

Where are all the Prophets?

Why is it, particularly in my branch of Christianity, that the prophets are all talking about such immediate issues? Where are the Josephs who dreamed 14 years into the future and saved both those around him (the Egyptians) and his own people (the Israelites)? When was the last time the Church had a Daniel who, through his deep wisdom and study of the scriptures, could see the time of dramatic cultural, political and spiritual change for his own people? Where are the Augustines[2] who had the clarity of thought

---

[2] Augustine wrote his famous work *The City of God* as an answer to the fears that the Church would fail as a result of the mighty Rome falling to the Visigoths in 410AD. They later withdrew but this event confused the faith of the Church in their mighty city. Augustine helped the Church see that it

and wisdom to guide the young Roman Church through its darkest hours of the barbarian invasions in the 5th Century?

The last time the Church was hearing a clarion call of the prophets was in the Y2K crisis. You remember those paper tigers. Back in 1999 the CBC (Canadian Broadcasting Corporation) had a weekly Y2K[3] bug report that kept us up to date as to how things were progressing toward preparations for the infamous "bug." At the end of every report the journalist would save a good five minutes to talk about what the flaming evangelical doomsayers were saying. They would have a nice chuckle as they pondered who the antichrist was; some were now saying it was Bill Gates, or when the rapture was going to take place. It was embarrassing. It made me want to revive the Old Testament practice of stoning false prophets or, at least, send them some really nasty computer virus.

I am not suggesting that this book is in any way a prophetic statement for the church and the future. If anything I am focusing on the enormous changes due to these new technologies in our present world. What I am trying to do in these pages is to start asking the right questions. If our world is changing, a notion we seem to have to prove to some, then how does this affect the way we live our Christian faith? Does it affect how we disciple? Does it affect how

---

was not based in an earthly political kingdom but one that proceeds from God.

[3] Y2K is the acronym for Year 2000. The bug in almost all computers was a problem with how we manage the dates in computer systems and programs. Instead of creating a date 01/01/2000 for January 1st, 2000 programmers and computer developers had been abbreviating the date since the early sixties so that this day would appear 01/01/00. Computers had no way of knowing as the new millennium click over on our digital machines whether we were in the year 2000 or 1900. Those of us who were now using computers for nearly everything were not sure if everything would shut down because our computer systems were confused. One group to profit incredibly from this problem was the very people who caused it, the computer industry. They did more business in 1999 than in the four years previous combined. We all had to upgrade. A quick Google search will still find out of date web pages warning us of the impending doom. What happened? Not much.

we raise our kids so that they will stay true to the faith? Should we be equipping our upcoming church leaders in ways that will prepare them for the changing cultural environment or is it good enough just to teach them how to use PowerPoint? Should we escape and head for the hills or should we engage and login?

This is not *Digital for Dummies*

This book is not about how to set up a website or the need to get a digital projector in the church so we can use PowerPoint for our songs instead of those annoying overhead transparencies. I am also not writing about discipleship techniques over the internet.

Chatting with a friend about what I was writing brought an interesting reaction. She commented, "I know that there is something to what you are saying but I am about 'real' relationships. I would rather see someone face to face." She misunderstood. She thought I was talking about using technology as the primary means of discipleship. Though I do this in a very significant way, being the principal of an online Christian school, this is not what I am trying to write about.

Yes, aspects of discipleship can be done through internet technologies similar to writing and sending a letter via the postman, or in the case of the Apostle Paul, via a messenger. I am sure if Paul had the technology of the telephone he would have been their biggest long distance customer. But, if you notice the title of this book, it is not about how to use technology to disciple, rather, it is about how to disciple in a world that uses technology. If something is powerful enough to change my life then it is important to know how to walk in and through it just as Jesus would walk in and through it. The useful WWJD bracelets need to be plastered all over our computer.

Is a Digital World Good or Bad?

I will do all that I can to resist the temptation toward making any ethical judgment on these new fangdangled technologies. It is easy to do. The unknown is a scary place. When one thinks of the danger and the amazing miracles that are wrapped up in these little electronic bits, one has to wonder, "Have we gone too far or has God been waiting for us to get here?"

The late Neil Postman has done a masterful job in his book, *Technopoly,* by helping us see the hidden dangers of trusting in technology. He writes in the book's introduction:

"...most people believe technology is a staunch friend. There are two reasons for this. First, technology *is* a friend. It makes life easier, cleaner and longer. Can anyone ask more of a friend? Second, because of its lengthy, intimate and inevitable relationship with culture, technology does not invite a close examination of its own consequences. It is the kind of friend that asks for trust and obedience, which most people are inclined to give because its gifts are truly bountiful. But, of course, there is a dark side to this friend. Its gifts are not without a heavy cost. Stated in the most dramatic terms, the accusation can be made that the uncontrolled growth of technology destroys the vital sources of our humanity. It creates a culture without a moral foundation. It undermines certain mental processes and social relations that make human life worth living. Technology, in sum, is both friend and enemy." [4]

Looking at the changes in our Digital World from a Christian perspective raises some interesting ideas.

First, isn't this capacity to harness God's creation evidence of our loving Creator and the complexity of His

---

[4] Neil Postman, *Technopoly: The Surrender of Culture to Technology*, New York, Vintage Books, 1993. Introduction.

Universe? Absolutely, but this doesn't necessarily justify the way we use it. I had an old friend try to make this argument years ago when he pleaded, "I think it is OK to smoke marijuana because God put the THC in the plants for us to find." No doubt that THC has amazing medicinal uses but so far we've used it to get very, very stoned. Yet, when we see the incredible forces of electricity harnessed to do all that our modern culture uses it for, it is hard not to praise the Creator of such wonderment.

Secondly, we cannot forget that man has fallen and has strayed far from God. One only has to look to the recent history of the last century to see how we can turn these miraculous powers to evil. The nuclear age was born from the bed of World Wars! We consoled ourselves in the Cold War with the doctrine of Mutual Assured Destruction[5] or aptly shortened to the acronym MAD. These global dangers were here because at the core of who we are, we have fallen from the noble creatures God made us to be.[6]

Finally, as Christians we are a bit aloof to the culture. I don't mean that we are to be indifferent but rather that we are truly not a part of this world. We have been called by God to live a new life that comes from a new and different world. Jesus indicated in His famous prayer of John 17 that *"these are in the world... not of the world"*.[7] In

---

[5] *Mutual assured destruction*, Wikipedia, The Free Encyclopedia. 4 April 2006 14:40 UTC. http://en.wikipedia.org/wiki/Mutual_assured_dest-ruction "The doctrine assumes that each side has enough weaponry to destroy the other side and that either side, if attacked for any reason by the other, would retaliate with equal or greater force. The expected result is an immediate escalation resulting in both combatants' total and assured destruction. It is now generally assumed that the nuclear fallout or nuclear winter would bring about worldwide devastation, though this was not a critical assumption to the theory of MAD."

[6] Genesis 2:17 (KJV) *But of the tree of the knowledge of good and evil, thou shalt not eat of it: for in the day that thou eatest thereof thou shalt surely die.*; Romans 3:23 (NIV) *for all have sinned and fall short of the glory of God,*; Romans 5:12 (NIV) *Therefore, just as sin entered the world through one man, and death through sin, and in this way death came to all men, because all sinned—*

[7] John 17:11,16 (KJV)

a sense, we are foreigners and aliens[8] to this old world and its culture. Therefore we are called to live apart from it or not to be affected by it. So, as we observe this world, we have a sense of detachment. Again, I am not calling for indifference. I think we need to fight with the best of them for a better world for our fellow man.

I have been and will be the first to carry the placard declaring "abortion is evil" and "same sex marriage is an abomination," but I do these things for my fellow man, not for the Christian or the Gospel's sake. I believe abortion is the taking of a human life which is sacred and I will stand up for that human. I believe homosexuality to be an abhorrent behavior that people choose, and for their good, I will resist this behavior. Again, I am aloof, not trying to persuade the Christian, but trying to persuade my fellow American or Canadian. So too, with the Digital World, it is the world we find ourselves in. It is the place where we are called to sojourn and carry on the commission of the Lord Jesus Christ. I am neither opposed to it nor for it. I am just here in it.

As stated before, when you read the following pages, my goal is to raise multiple questions. Andrew Shearman, from our Church's pulpit, aptly put it years ago: "Christians today are answering questions nobody is asking." I will take this thought a bit further: "Christians today are answering questions that have no relevance to the changes our culture is undergoing." Or, "Christians today are answering questions that should have been asked fifty years ago." We are working on problems in our society that began thirty to fifty years ago at the theoretical level. If we had been on our toes in the fifties and the sixties, perhaps we could have diverted such problems as abortion and same-sex marriages.

---

[8] 1 Peter 2:11 (NIV) *Dear friends, I urge you, as aliens and strangers in the world, to abstain from sinful desires, which war against your soul.*; Colossians 3:1-4 (NIV) *Since, then, you have been raised with Christ, set your hearts on things above, where Christ is seated at the right hand of God. Set your minds on things above, not on earthly things. For you died, and your life is now hidden with Christ in God. When Christ, who is your life, appears, then you also will appear with him in glory.*

If we had not abdicated key cultural positions, perhaps we could have been more of an influence on the tumultuous upheaval in our culture that has thrust us headlong into a postmodern tailspin.

If we will start asking the right questions, perhaps we will start finding the right answers - the Jesus inspired answers. We can then begin preparing our churches, our leaders, our educators, our parents and especially, our children. I believe we will then have a place at the table in this new Digital World!

This book is intended to jump-start this process. I do not anticipate many answers coming out of what I am writing, mostly questions. I will give, in nearly all of the chapters, some of the history related to each topic. My purpose is to give context to phenomenon that we are witnessing today. I have always believed that the roadmap to the future is in the past.

Section One, *Understanding the Concepts,* unveils God's digital signature in creation and how our technology can now decipher this Digital World. Discover the commis sion, context and curriculum of discipleship from primitive, Amazonian Indians, reality TV and sci-fi aliens.

Section Two, *The Four Digital Transformations,* reveals the blessings and curses of the new Digital World. In *Communication Revolution* see how we are experiencing a "Gutenberg-ian" moment of destiny that will eclipse the Reformation. In *Globalization,* from the pages of Genesis to the technological "flattening" of our world, see the tsunami-like cultural shifts. *Informationalism* unveils the vast alterations to society because the world's information is being placed at our fingertips. In *Biotechnology* see the implications of genetic manipulation, stem cell research, cloning and the merger of computers to our very selves.

Section Three, *The Digital Future,* shows all four of these transformations moving at an exponential rate. The book closes with two visions of the future: *The Enhanced Future* where technology continues to bless and enhance our human experience or *The Deprived Future* where our digital culture cascades into discrimination and servitude, devaluing and undermining our very existence. Will it be grim or bright? Will it be day or night? What will be their ethical challenges?

What would Jesus do in 2056?

Section One

Understanding the Concepts

"Become a student of change. It is the only thing that will remain constant."

Anthony J. D'Angelo,
The College Blue Book

What is so "Digital" about this World?

Swift as a shadow, short as any dream;
Brief as the lightning in the collied night
That, in a spleen, unfolds both heaven and earth,
And ere a man hath power to say "Behold!"
The jaws of darkness do devour it up:
So quick bright things come to confusion.
William Shakespeare[9]

God has created an invisible digital power inside of every thing in our universe and we have only begun to tap the surface of what this means. Since the infusing moment when God pronounced, *"Let there be light,"*[10] our universe has been held together by the unifying force of electricity. Consider the miracle of the electro-magnetic fields that hold everything together. Without these little atomic particles, so small that our most powerful microscopes cannot begin to unveil their presence, everything would fly apart into space at the sub-atomic level. Could it be that this is the

---

[9] William Shakespeare, *A Midsummer Nights Dream*. Act 1, Scene 1, Lines 141-149. Spoken by Lysander in discussion with Hermia about the intense force of love. We can easily see these Shakespearean lines suitably used for the amazing power of electricity. Alas, Shakespeare died 100 years before its discovery. What prose would have flowed had he known.
[10] Genesis 1:3 (NIV)

point where creation meets the word of His power; *"...and upholding all things by the word of his power,..."* [11] Is this magical electron where the physical meets the spiritual? Scriptures teach that one day, when God is finished with this physical universe and is ready to start a *"...new heavens and a new earth wherein dwelleth righteousness,"*[12] He will cause the old one to melt with fervent heat. Peter's apocalyptic vision describes this event with a sense of terror: *"Looking for and hasting unto the coming of the day of God, wherein the heavens being on fire shall be dissolved, and the elements shall melt with fervent heat."*[13] Could this be the moment when He removes His invisible, holding force upon the electrons and allows them to fly indiscriminately into every direction, instantaneously dissolving all matter? If this is true then the electron connects us to the mystery and majesty of God's creative pattern. This would mean God's creative pattern is digital.

In the book "Electric Universe," David Bodanis describes the mystifying activity of electrons:

"In the 20th Century the door opened even further. A few physicists were finally able to look directly at the face of electricity. The younger ones were awed by what they saw. Many of the older ones, including even the great Einstein, pulled back saying that what this now revealed was something they could never accept. What the researchers had found was the atoms inside us don't really look like miniature solar systems with electrons orbiting like miniature planets around a tiny sun. Rather, these electrons, which are central to how electricity affects us, can wildly teleport from one location to another. It was the only partially predictable nature of these jumps that Einstein was thinking of when he famously said, 'God does not

---

[11] Hebrews 1:3 (KJV) – this important passage teaches that Jesus, the Word made flesh, possesses a preeminent place in the universe and his very spoken word is the power that holds all things together.

[12] 2 Peter 3:13 (KJV)

[13] 2 Peter 3:12 (KJV)

play dice with the universe.' And it was to that dictum that his friend Neils Bohr exasperatedly replied, 'Einstein stop telling God what to do!' That jumping of electrons within us would be as if the earth were an electron that could instantly shoot away from the sun and take up a position hovering above the planet Jupiter...."[14]

The simple digital signals, + or −, find their way into every aspect of matter and life itself. From the coldest inanimate object in the farthest reaches of space to the DNA molecule, our universe is governed by digital signatures and signals. Everything, everywhere is digital.

The First Digital Electronic Communication

It has only been a relatively short two hundred years since we have had the ability to manipulate electricity and unlock the digital value of this rarely seen force.

It was in 1826 that Joseph Henry, a jack-of-all-trades, found himself doing the unpleasant rustic work of a surveyor close to the Canadian border. The wilderness and cold were enough to convince Joseph that he had to find another occupation. An opportunity became available to teach math and science to elementary age boys in Albany, New York and thus started Joseph Henry's long and distinguished career as an educator. As any experienced teacher will tell you, keeping the attention of twenty or so eleven year old boys cooped up in a winter schoolhouse is no easy task. He had to find something interesting that would occupy their restless yet inquisitive minds.

Joseph kept himself informed of the latest in scientific and technological research and development. The latest

---

[14] David Bodanis, *Electric Universe: The Shocking True Story of Electricity.* Crown Publishing, 2005. This has proven to be an excellent resource in understanding how electricity has been used over the last two hundred years written in layman's terms. He has captured the human side of this historical journey.

scientific fad was to manipulate and experiment with the unpredictable yet exciting force of electricity, something in which famous Philadelphian Benjamin Franklin had some renown. Joseph read about the recent experiments of Englishman William Sturgeon who, through a great deal of tinkering, discovered that if you wrap copper wire around iron and connect it to a battery, the iron becomes magnetized.[15] Switch off the battery and it returns to simple iron.

Joseph knew that this would create an exciting science project for his boys and within six months they were able to duplicate Sturgeon's effects with an electro-magnet that could lift ten pounds. He and his students continued with their experiments until they were able to lift astonishing weights of up to 1500 pounds. Joseph, a passionate Christian, would explain to his students, and his growing following, that God had placed these invisible forces within our universe for man to discover and use for His glory.[16]

Joseph and his boys continued to tinker with their new discovery. If they lengthened the wire between the battery and the magnet they still could achieve similar effects as long as the wire wasn't too long. From a different location they could make the magnet turn on and off and ring a bell (this most likely became an excellent boyish prank on some unsuspecting teacher or student in the next room). This led Joseph to the idea that perhaps one could communicate remotely through the use of electro-magnets. He developed a small magnetic tapper that would move up and down and create a clicking sound when the battery was

---

[15] Alexander Volta (1745-1827) invented the first batteries by placing two dissimilar metals in a tube (cell) separated by a gap and then filled with brine. This invention is made even more remarkable by the fact that there was almost no reason to store an electrical charge in his time.

[16] At the end of Henry's life he is quoted as saying: "God has created man in his own intellectual image, and graciously permitted him to study His modes of operation, and rewards his industry in this line by giving him powers and instruments which affect in the highest degree his material welfare." Remarks given at the Laying of the Cornerstone of the American Museum of Natural History (New York), June 2, 1874: Arthur P. Molella, et al., eds., *A Scientist in American Life: Essays and Lectures of Joseph Henry.* Washington, D.C., 1980, p. 115.

turned on and off. By putting a sequence of clicks together he could communicate certain letters. With this very simple idea Joseph Henry and his group of elementary school boys experienced the first form of electronic digital communication.[17]

By 1832, Joseph Henry had taken a position at Princeton University and continued his research building on his earlier experiments with electro-magnets.

Progress was being made in London where a mile-long line was stretched between train stops to communicate arrivals and departures.

The eccentric Henry Morse found Joseph at Princeton and, perhaps not with the greatest integrity, learned enough about Joseph's invention to create his own telegraph (he patented it as his own invention). Though he wasn't really responsible for the invention of the telegraph he did become the name's sake of the new digital language being used exclusively by the telegraph. For the next one hundred and fifty years, Morse code became the first truly digital language using the same binary concept, on or off, which is the foundation of all our digital marvels today.

Digital Communication Changes Everything

Henry and Morse were the first to use digital technology but what is more astounding is how it dramatically changed culture, relationships, commerce, politics, geography and pushed us into a strange symbiosis of technology and human experience. Consider that any and all communication before the invention of the telegraph was no quicker than the fastest human messenger. Communicating a simple message like, "We have negotiated peace with our enemy," could take days, weeks and even months depending

---

[17] This is the account of the first time "electronic digital communication" occurred but the first forms of digital communication came long before the discovery of electricity. Probably the first long distance form of digital communication would have been the simple on and off messaging created between two distant tribes through smoke signals.

on the distance involved. Treaties and agreements were often reached weeks or months before the battles and conflicts ceased. Great gains or loses on the battle field were instantly nullified when the messenger arrived.

Elaborate systems of communication travel such as the "Pony Express" were developed to speed the messenger. The fastest, sleekest ships on the ocean often became the first target in times of war. Scientific innovation and progress was impeded and often duplicated in other parts of the world. This meant waiting months and often years for publication to circulate. This is even the case of the telegraph that was worked on in Britain, Germany and the US all at the same time.

The highest consistent speed of travel in 1840 was the trains, reaching breakneck velocities of 30 mph. Ship travel was about two thirds this speed but far less reliable. At these speeds, a message from London to New York was still a week away, as long as the weather cooperated. Consider the response time of a government, business or family when news takes so long. Your loved ones could have passed away months ago and you wouldn't be the wiser. Disasters could strike at distant outposts. Fortunes could have been won in other parts of the world. Economies rise and fall before news of any change. Kings are displaced, presidents elected, governments overthrown, armies mobilized before word travels to your distant shores. All of this was changed by the simple on/off click made by a battery, a magnet and a wire.

The New Emerging Technology

The emergence of digital technology was a bit slow by today's standards. One could think of it as the first half of an exponential curve, a curve where we find ourselves at the later quarter in the extreme climb toward acceleration. Telegraph systems began showing up around 1840 and the first successful transatlantic cable was completed in 1866. It took another forty years before wireless telegraphy was discovered, which created a whole new wave of technological advancement.

Communication research and development took a different turn in the late 1800's toward "analog" technology with the inventions of the microphone, speaker, telephone, gramophone, and later on, television.

Analog technology is one step from digital technology. Analog signals are not true digital signals because they rely on waves and pressure to reproduce the sounds or images. An analog signal translates the sound waves into an electrical wave signal that emulates the sound wave and then retranslates it back into sound waves at the speaker output. Digital technology takes those electronic analog waves and translates it further into digital code. The code is then sent down the wire or across the airwaves and retranslated at the destination point to an electronic analog and then back to the original medium. In any analog system, there is a great deal of degradation and corruption of the signal as it is transported along the wire or airwaves. Recording an analog signal also becomes a challenge as it will only last as long as the medium lasts, such as a vinyl record disk or magnetic cassette tape. In recording and storing digital content there are great advantages over analog. There is virtually no degradation in the storage of digital content and it will last as long as the laws of physics rule the universe or until your hard drive crashes.

The exciting thing about developing analog technology in the first half of the last century was the depth of communication becoming available. People could hold verbal conversations as opposed to cryptic digital code being sent through a telegraph operator. The telegraph communication was far more efficient but it required the additional translation from an analog to a digital message and back to analog again. Eventually, the same physics of sound were applied to video and the television was invented. It wasn't until the invention of the transistor that digital technology began to re-emerge as the medium of choice.

The Digital Switch

The transistor,[18] a sort of an electronic switch, routed the electronic signals to different locations and outputs depending on the variation of on-s and off-s in the signal.

One long and boring summer in my middle school years, my mother convinced me to take a summer school class. Actually, I must have committed some dastardly junior high school deed and was given this ultimatum. There was a computer math class offered at the beginning level or at least the teacher was trying to bring it to this level. In the class I was introduced to the concept of the Base 2 Numerical System.[19] I didn't make it through the class but I did last long enough to learn that there is a number system completely made up of zeros and ones (0000 and 1111). Depending on how these are arranged determines the values granted to the "byte" of information. There it was, on or off, zero or one. Stated as a complete over-simplification, these

---

[18] *Transistors.* Wikipedia, The Free Encyclopedia. 1 April 2006 22:12 UTC http://en.wikipedia.org/wiki/Transistor "Transistors have three terminals where, in simplified terms, the application of voltage to the input terminal increases the conductivity between the other two terminals and hence controls current flow through those terminals. ..... In analog circuits, transistors are used in amplifiers, audio amplifiers, radio frequency amplifiers, regulated power supplies, and in computer PSUs, especially in switching power supplies. Transistors are also used in digital circuits where they function similarly to electrical switches. Digital circuits include logic gates, RAM (random access memory) and microprocessors."

[19] Base 2 is also known as the Binary Numerical System. *Binary numeral system.* Wikipedia, The Free Encyclopedia. 5 April 2006 09:54 UTC http://en.wikipedia.org/wiki/Base_2 "The **binary numeral system** represents numeric values using two symbols, typically 0 and 1. More specifically, binary is a positional notation with a radix of two. Owing to its relatively straightforward implementation in electronic circuitry, the binary system is used internally by virtually all modern computers."

zeros and ones are the way electricity can be turned into the wondrous and mysterious feats of computer technology by being routed through transistors. The typical Microprocessor chip created in 2005 is made up of about 287 million transistors.

With the invention of the transistor in the late 40's and the discovery of the magical conductive properties of silicon in the 50's, the modern computer age was born.

Transistors, or as I like to think of them, "digital switches," are now a part of every aspect of our lives. In my own home we could have as many as a billion transistors. We are somewhat of a geekie family in that everyone in the home has their own networked computer. This would be six running computers: four are wireless notebooks and two PCs, and we have two or three computers waiting for repairs at any given time. Added to the computer device list are two printers, network and wifi hubs, an Xbox game console, 2 Ipods, 2 MP3 players, my pocket PC and 3 cell phones. Transistors are also found in our 3 TVs, microwave, remote phone system, DVD player, VCR, refrigerator, clocks, and nearly every other device that uses electricity in a controlled way. Consider that this minute digital switch was invented less than sixty years ago and almost a billion of them, albeit mostly in the computers, have invaded my middle class, North American home.

Digital Ubiquity

The first time I heard this word was at a computer convention back in the early 90's. I heard three different speakers on several occasions speak about the *ubiquitous*[20] nature of their specific applications. One of the references was to the internet. Most of the listening audience

---

[20] "Being or seeming to be everywhere at the same time; omnipresent: 'plodded through the shadows fruitlessly like an ubiquitous spook' (Joseph Heller)." *The American Heritage® Dictionary of the English Language, Fourth Edition.* Houghton Mifflin Company, 2000. Found at Dictonary.com (http://dictionary.reference.com/search?q=ubiquitous)

squirmed with a bit of skepticism when he said, "the internet will become the ubiquitous tool of everyday life."

Digital-ness is a reality that can certainly be thought of as omnipresent. The digital nature of atomic structure means that everything has a digital signature. But now, with the advent of the electronic discoveries, inventions and the computer, digital ubiquity is a fact of life in the new millennium.

When a technology is thought of as ubiquitous it integrates with everything and becomes invisible. The example of a billion transistors in my home reveals this. As our culture continues to embrace and explore this new frontier of discovery, we will integrate our very selves into digital-ness. Alas, it is already happening. Consider how natural it is for you to flow through digital portals of life in the new millennium: banking, listing to music, watching TV, taking medicine, picking up the phone, driving to school, messaging a friend, downloading a song, buying a book, changing the thermostat, checking stock prices, checking the weather, reheating your food, and googling the word ubiquitous.

It seems almost silly to have to make the case that North American culture is rushing into digital-ness. Even our churches are trying, as fast as we can with our limited resources, to become digital places of worship. Think about the last time you were in a church without a digital projector. In most of our churches we spend three or four times more on technology than we do on our children's programs. It is not a good day to drop into the Pastor's office when the church's internet server is having issues.

Neil Postman helps us understand the all encompassing nature of technology. He gives us somewhat of a grim view of how we become the subject of the very technological tools we have invented:

"In a technocracy, tools play a central role in the thought-world of the culture. Everything must give way, in some degree, to their development. The social and symbolic world become increasingly subject to the requirements of that development. Tools are not integrated into the culture, they attack the culture; they bid to become the culture. As a consequence tradition, social mores, myth, politics, ritual and religion have to fight for their lives."[21]

Note the phrase, "they (the technological tools) bid to become the culture." The entire thesis of his book is that our culture is becoming a *"Techonopoly"* meaning, we are here to serve the advancement of technology and not the other way around. Isn't this what was meant when Marshall McLuhan coined the phrase "the medium is the message?"[22] The "medium" are those things we use to extend ourselves beyond ourselves like the telegraph or the computer. The message is not really the content we are trying to send or convey but rather the medium itself. I am writing this book about a digital world and how it affects everything about who we are. The digital technology has become the message and we find ourselves subtly serving this message in every aspect of our lives.

Because the medium has become so pervasive, so ubiquitous, we fail to see its effects. "It's like the fish in the water, we don't know who discovered water but we know it wasn't a fish. A pervasive medium is always beyond perception."[23] McLuhan.

Central to our Judeo-Christian ethic is the command *"You shall have no other gods before me. You shall not make for yourself an idol in the form of anything in heaven above or on the earth beneath or in the waters below. You shall not bow down to them or worship them; for I, the LORD your*

---

[21] Neil Postman, *Technopoly: The Surrender of Culture to Technology*, New York, Vintage Books, 1993.

[22] Marshall McLuhan and Quentin Fiore. *The Medium is the Massage: An Inventory of Effects*. Gingko Press, 2000. McLuhn, Canadian born, became the foremost critic and professor of media studies in the last half of the 20th century. He argued that the tactile, all embracing effects of electric media will undo the linear, civilizing effects of phonetic alphabet and print.

[23] Ibid.

God, am a jealous God,..."[24] Have we subtly made this new digital culture a form of idolatry? Is our striving for the next technological wonder or solution a sign of our idolatry?

Moore's Law

Gordon E. Moore was a co-founder of the technology giant Intel. More than half of all computer chips in the world come from his company. In 1965, Moore observed that the rate of our technological development was doubling every 18 months.[25] In 1975, he expanded this prediction of doubling to every 24 months. He based this "law" on the amount of transistors that can be put on a computer chip at relatively the same size and cost. It has continued to hold true to this day. Every two years, computer power has continued to double and this pace doesn't seem to be slowing any time soon.

My brother-in-law is an engineer for Intel. He manages several groups of programmers and designers who use powerful computers to write programs for the computers that make the computer chip. He refers to the development of the computer chip as a magic that only a few people on the planet really understand. Even the wizards of this new technology need computers to help the evolution of the next level of chip development. We need computers to make the computers that make the computers!

---

[24] Exodus 20: 3-5 (NIV)

[25] *Moore's law.* Wikipedia, The Free Encyclopedia. 5 April 2006 08:27 UTC http://en.wikipedia.org/wiki/Moore's_law "Moore's original statement can be found in his publication "Cramming more components onto integrated circuits", *Electronics Magazine* 19 April 1965: 'The complexity for minimum component costs has increased at a rate of roughly a factor of two per year ... Certainly over the short term this rate can be expected to continue, if not to increase. Over the longer term, the rate of increase is a bit more uncertain, although there is no reason to believe it will not remain nearly constant for at least 10 years. That means by 1975, the number of components per integrated circuit for minimum cost will be 65,000. I believe that such a large circuit can be built on a single wafer.'"

Computer companies are working on what is called *nanotechnology*[26] to work at a deeper microscopic level of chip building that will make transistors at the molecular level. Moore predicted that the doubling will have to slow down eventually since transistors may reach the limits of miniaturization at the atomic level. We aren't quite there yet but it is getting close.

One question we have to start asking is, 'how far will this all go?' Joel Garreau, reporter and editor at the Washington Post, writes in his latest book, *Radical Evolution:*

> "Four interrelated, intertwining technologies are cranking up to modify human nature. Call them the GRIN technologies - the genetic, robotic, information and nano processes. These four advances are intermingling and feeding on one another, and they are collectively creating a curve of change unlike anything we humans have ever seen." [27]

There is no question we have entered the Digital Age with challenges and changes no man has ever imagined. It is clear that we will continue on this path of evolving technology until we reach some catastrophic end or run out of silicon.[28] Our Christian faith has weathered many storms throughout the last two millennium but how do we prepare for what's coming: the integration of man and machine, the connection of the human psyche to the vast resources of the internet, technologies that work at the atomic level and the new art form of genetic manipulation? Are we searching for the right answers in scripture? Are we able to give guidance to our sons and daughters in university today? How about

---

[26]*Nanotchnology.* Wikipedia, The Free Encyclopedia. 5 April 2006 15:57 UTC http://en.wikipedia.org/wiki/Nanotechnology Nanotechnology is any technology which exploits phenomena and structures that can only occur at the nanometer scale, which is the scale of single atoms and small molecules.
[27] Joel Garreau, *Radical Evolution: The Promise and Peril of Enhancing our Minds, our Bodies-and what it means to be Human.* Random House, 2005. pg. 4.
[28] Note that silicone is the second most abundant element on the planet.

the universities of tomorrow? Are our pulpits preparing us to live in a world of robots, genetic alteration and unlimited information? What would Jesus do in a digital world?

"But sanctify the Lord God in your hearts: and be ready always to give an answer to every man that asketh you a reason of the hope that is in you with meekness and fear:"
1 Peter 3:15 (KJV)

Discipleship: The Biggest Word in Christianity

"The Church in North America is diminishing because we are raising converts not kings."[29]

Brodie Kalamen

Jesus has died and risen from the dead. He leaves for several weeks and then returns again to spend considerable time with His disciples in their home town by the sea of Galilee. They enjoy wonderful fellowship with the risen Lord eating and sharing together. He teaches and explains many things to them. They ask Him if He is going to establish His kingdom on earth now and He gently reminds them that this is not the time, but to go back to Jerusalem and wait for the promised coming of the Holy Spirit.[30] On one of His final days He invites His eleven disciples (Judas was obviously not there) to meet and walk with Him up one of

---

[29] Brodie Kalamen is the youth pastor at the Kelowna Christian Center. He made this comment in a Sunday Sermon entitled *"Heavenly Inheritance,"* March 5th, 2006. You can download many of his sermons at www.kcc.net .

[30] John 21:1-24 and Acts 1:1-8

the local hills.[31] It is there that He gives them some of His very last recorded words on earth.

Imagine speaking to your loved ones in this context. What would you say if you knew the very next sentences would be the last words they would hear from you for the rest of their natural lives? Would you not weigh these words? Would you not want to leave them with some lasting bit of instruction, exhortation or comfort? These would, undoubtedly, be the most important things you would ever say to your loved ones.

The Gospel of Matthew records for us one of the very last statements[32] Jesus made to His eleven disciples. These words carry the weight of a "last will and testament." Jesus gave these words the weight of finality. They can be thought of as the biggest words of Christianity. This is why the traditional summary of this passage is aptly called "The Great Commission."

"Then Jesus came to them and said, "All authority in heaven and on earth has been given to me. Therefore go and make disciples of all nations, baptizing them in the name of the Father and of the Son and of the Holy Spirit, and teaching them to obey everything I have commanded you. And surely I am with you always, to the very end of the age."
Matthew 28:18-20 (NIV)

This commission must become the central motivation for all we do inside and outside of the church. It was the last directive that Jesus gave the disciples and must be the defining activity of all Christian experience. It takes

---

[31] The scripture uses the word "mountain." Being a resident of British Columbia and having visited Israel and seen the true stature of their mountains, the word *hill* gives the correct impression.

[32] It is clear that this meeting with the disciples spoken of in Mathew 28:16-20 was probably not the very last time he met with the disciples. The commission was given in Galilee and the last time Jesus was seen was on the Mount of Olives after he implores the disciples to stay in Jerusalem: Acts 1:11-12. Clearly, Matthew's Gospel presents the "Great Commission" as the very last statement of Jesus thus giving it the "last will and testament" status.

within it all the stages of Christian growth from pre-conversion to full-grown maturity in Christ.[33]

God is a Green Light

A good friend and teacher in my Bible School days coined the phrase, "God is a green light." He would almost always continue to rant, "The last thing Jesus told us to do is go. He didn't say pray about going. He didn't say think about going. He said, 'Go.'" My friend would then, in his dramatic and almost maniacal style, begin to shout at us, "Go! Go! Go in the name of Jesus! GO!" Needless to say it did tend to quickly end the Bible study.

One young missionary, Bruce Olson,[34] did just that in 1961. At the tender age of nineteen, he heard the call of Matthew 28:18-20 and bought a one-way ticket to Venezuela leaving his family and friends in Minnesota. With almost no money, no official missionary connections and no experience, Bruce set out to reach the most remote tribe in the Amazon, the Motilone.

No white man had survived contact with this group of Indians in 400 years since the Spanish Conquistadors. As Bruce approached their territory, he was shot in the leg with a poison arrow and taken prisoner. The wound became infected forcing Bruce to escape his captors and make his way out of the jungle to get medical attention. Undaunted by this affliction, he returned to Motilone territory and again was captured. This time during his captivity he came

---

[33] Discipleship is often spoken of as just the process of teaching believers and not that it begins with taking the Gospel to the nations. I have documented seven stages of spiritual development based upon Matt. 28:19, Hebrews 5:11-14 and 1 John 2:12-14. They are pre-conversion; conversion; babyhood; childhood-adolescence; young adulthood, mature-adulthood and fatherhood.

[34] The story of Bruce Olson is told in the epic missions' story of how he came to the Motilone people, *Bruchko*. I consider this to be a must read for anyone thinking about going into Cross Cultural Missions. Bruce Olson. *Bruchko*. Charisma House, June 1977. You can learn more about the amazing Bruce Olson at the web site: www.bruceolson.com.

down with hepatitis. A helicopter saw his distress signal and rescued him. Courageously, he returned for a third time. This time the Indians believed that he was God-sent because of the "big metal bird" which had rescued him. After living and working with these unique, tree dwelling people for many years, Bruce was able to reach them with the gospel message: Jesus came to redeem them from sin and give them a new life with God. In time, the entire tribe embraced this message.

The gospel not only brought spiritual reform to these people but it also transformed how they viewed their place in the world. The Motilones are now some of the most progressive, academic and giving native people in all of South America. The tribe has sent a small army of young people off to Secondary and Post Secondary Institutes to receive education in the fields of medicine and language as well as vocational training. Bruce has built facilities and trained people to work in eighteen health centers, forty-two bilingual schools, twenty-two agricultural centers, and eleven trading posts which function as co-ops.

The Motilone have sparked social development in places overlooked by the governments of Colombia and Venezuela. The co-operatives provide the economic base for eighteen tribal people groups. The director of the Bureau of Indian Affairs for Northeast Colombia is a Motilone lawyer. The director of Indian Affairs for the state government is a Motilone graduate of business administration. The coordinator for press relations for Northeast Colombia Native Peoples' Affairs is a Motilone university graduate of journalism.

Obviously, Bruce Olson took seriously the idea that Jesus conveyed: our responsibility to get outside of our own community and make disciples. He tells us to "make disciples of all nations" or people groups. He intends for us, based on His universal authority, to proselytize, evangelize, indoctrinate and completely convert every nation and people group to Christianity.

Becoming All Things To All People

In order for Bruce Olson to effectively reach the Motilone people he had to learn their language and culture. He had to, in a sense, become a Motilone. This is probably the greatest lesson we can learn from Bruce's story. When he first arrived in Venezuela he visited a missions' outpost on the edge of the vast Amazon forest. The few native converts all looked and dressed in western clothing. Their own people rejected them because they embraced not only a foreign god but also had to become foreigners in their dress and actions. It was here that Bruce's simple philosophy of missions was established. He correctly saw his mission to convert the Indians to Christ, not to westernize them. By embracing Motilone culture he showed them that Jesus wanted to be a Motilone, that Jesus loved the Motilones so much that he was willing to become a Motilone.

Faith Annette Sand, former assistant editor of *Missiology* magazine, visited Bruce Olson in the Amazon and writes on his website:

"When he first went to South America, Bruce's well-to-do family and various mission organizations expressed distress at his intentions. He was told he had neither the education nor the experience to prepare him for such a venture. And when Bruce responded that he knew God was leading him to do this, they were angered by his insolence. Today, [thirty-eight years later,] Bruce has become a legend.

"What amazes missiologists is that countless missionaries around the world are being accused of destroying indigenous cultures or of making tribal peoples objects of idle curiosity. Yet someone like Bruce, with so little anthropological, theological, and cross-cultural training, has done so many things so correctly! (Seldom do the 'called' pan out so well.)

"Personally, I wonder if in this case his lack of preparation didn't help. Bruce was able to enter Motilone territory without preconceived or traditional ideas on how to go about evangelizing a tribal people. Of necessity, he had to be sensitive to the tribe and its culture -- and sensitive to the leading of the Holy Spirit."[35]

Obviously, I am writing about how to engage a new culture, a digital culture, whose language and practices are evolving into something very different than what we have come to know in our "enlightened western culture." In order to reach a digital culture we must, like Bruce Olson, become a part of this digital culture. Whereas Bruce had to return to a more primitive approach toward life, we must launch forward into the culture of a high-tech digital environment. We must learn to speak the language of this culture and communicate in such a way that the people will see that Jesus wants to become one of them. We must engage this culture in such a way that we become an integral part of it, that we help it, and find ways to serve within it.

When Faith Sand met Bruce for the first time she wrote of their conversation:

"The disparity between Bruce's tall Nordic frame, and the short, sturdy indigenous Motilones was the first thing I noticed. Yet his ease in communication with them and their naturalness with him somehow made him fit into their world.

"'You feel like a Motilone to me,' I said as we walked toward the house.

"'I will never really be a Motilone,' he answered. 'I will always be different from them. Yet I know I will never again feel fully comfortable in the culture where I was raised.'

"After having spent eighteen years in Latin America, I could relate to these feelings. To become a

---

[35] Faith Annette Sand *The Motilone (Barí) Miracle* http://www.bruceolson.com/english/texts/miracle1.html "*Faith Sand [former] assistant editor of Missiology, visited Bruce Olsson on assignment for the Other Side.*"

missionary is to give up not only the homeland but also the feeling of belonging in the homeland."[36]

The apostle Paul gives us clear insight into this necessary principle of discipleship in 1 Corinthians 9:19-23:

Even though I am free of the demands and expectations of everyone, I have voluntarily become a servant to any and all in order to reach a wide range of people: religious, nonreligious, meticulous moralists, loose-living immoralists, the defeated, the demoralized--whoever. I didn't take on their way of life. I kept my bearings in Christ--but I entered their world and tried to experience things from their point of view. I've become just about every sort of servant there is in my attempts to lead those I meet into a God-saved life. I did all this because of the Message. I didn't just want to talk about it; I wanted to be in on it![37]

In order for us to reach those in the various strata of culture we must "enter their world" and "experience things from their point of view." The call to be a part of the world has its root in our desire to serve the Message or as the New International Version translates verse 23, *"I do all this for the sake of the gospel.* [38]*"* In order to serve the gospel and the people we are called to reach, we must learn to speak their language. We must learn to embrace their culture. We must become one of them. Just as Jesus was able to become a Motilone through Bruce Olson, He wants to become a member of the new digital culture through those who are called to reach this generation.

Note that Paul had very few limits to the cultural persona that he would identify with in order to reach a wide range of people. He was willing to give away his Jewish distinctiveness in order to reach the non-Jewish culture of the Roman Empire. There was one aspect that he was unwilling to compromise. He states his non-negotiable moral position

---

[36] Ibid.
[37] (The Message Version)
[38] 1 Corinthians 9:23 (NIV)

in verse 21, *"To those not having the law I became like one not having the law (though I am not free from God's law but am under Christ's law), so as to win those not having the law."*[39] Paul was unwilling to let go of his conscience and commitment to Christ in order to reach a culture. In other words, he would do whatever it took to identify with the people he was trying to disciple except enter into sin.

This is the dangerous part of evangelism and discipleship. This is the part where we leave behind the safe moorings of our Christian traditions and etiquette. We must identify so closely with those we are called to reach that when others see us they will think we are one of them. The dangers, of course, are that we might actually lose ourselves in the culture and forget why we are there. On top of this, every missionary with a family recognizes the great risk they expose their children to. "I can go and identify with this culture but how will I keep my children from being affected by those we are trying to reach?" This also begs the questions: "Are not my own children instruments of Jesus as well?" "Will He not use them to reach this new culture?"

I have often felt that if there was no "Great Commission" then the Amish have got it right. Their disconnection with the worldly culture outside of their own community is inspired by a desire to see their children protected and their Christian, Anabaptist traditions continue.

Amish in the City

In the 2004 season and the rush to get the most controversial "reality TV" series, NBC aired ten episodes of "Amish in the City." The contrived "reality" circumstances brought five young people from several Amish communities together with five "average," secular, urban young people and put them in morally challenging situations. The Amish

---

[39] 1 Corinthians 9:21 (NIV)

have a fascinating tradition called *rumspringa*[40] in which the community encourages their young people to leave the moral shelter of their sequestered culture. They are sent into "the world" to decide which life they want to choose: the exciting, technological, glitzy cities and people or the quiet, simple, moral farming life of their Christian communal living. This event in the Amish young person's life is said to settle the choice once for all. If they return then their "rumspringa" experience is all forgiven and put behind them. If they don't return they have made their choice for the world, and the community lets them go.

The program was set in the heart of Los Angles and exposed these kids to all manner of Hollywood voyeurism. It was obvious that the producers of the show were trying to push the Amish kids into embracing some sort of modern enlightenment through technology, glitter, glitz and sin.

After watching a few episodes I saw something entirely unexpected. The Amish young people were surprised by the life styles and all that the city had to offer. But the effects of these revelations didn't move them as quickly to reject their Amish lifestyle as you might think. What stood out was something any casual viewer would have seen: the contrast of the solid character and peace of the Amish kids versus the undisciplined, immoral character of the secular kids. In fact, several of them began to regret their contemporary, liberal upbringing.

Let me say again, I am convinced that if Jesus had not given us the Great Commission the Amish have got it right. If we were not called to this missionary vocation then we should create some sequestered environment to raise our children safe from the dangers of a digital world. Why embrace a world that is so contrary to the nature and spirit

---

[40] Rumspringa has several interpretations. The idea that the kids are completely turned loose is more of a myth than fact. In most cases the kids are still at home with their parents and are allowed some various freedoms that help in their decision for baptism. Only a small majority completely leave their communities. Statistics bear this out with almost 90% of young adults returning to their Amish community and receiving baptism. For more info on "rumspringa" see: http://en.wikipedia.org/wiki/Rumspringa.

of the Christian life? Why risk the most important and precious lives given to our stewardship? Why care about a
world that is so bent on leading our children away from our
values and beliefs? Why? Because we are called to love that
which God loves. If God loves the people of this world, then
we are to love the people of this world. I want to love what
God loves and hate what God hates.

Clearly, there are things that God hates about our
world. There are many things humanity has done with our
world, His creation, motivated by our fallen-ness, which
God hates. There are aspects of the digital world that have
and will facilitate sinful behavior like never before. Consider that much of our technological innovation is a result
of finding better ways to kill each other. It is no secret that
the military is the primary financier of such innovation.
Even the internet can trace its beginnings to Arpanet - a
system designed to protect the US Department of Defense's
information during the dangerous cold war era. The potential to unleash upon the world such evil through technological means has never been on such a broad scale. The most
obvious dangers to our lives and cultures have been amplified by the internet: pornography, digital sex, pedophilia,
terrorist networks, online gambling, criminal activity and
the like. The innovation of all of these technologies facilitates greater platforms for our fallen-ness to spread and
grow.

So why engage, why login and why participate? Why
not adopt an Amish approach?

Aliens in this World

Being a Christian means that our spiritual nature is
alien to this world. Our in Christ[41] experience creates
within us revulsion for the fallen-ness that we still experience in our lives affected by the world. I will be the first to

---

[41] 2 Corinthians 5:17 (KJV) *Therefore if any man be in Christ, he is a new
creature: old things are passed away; behold, all things are become new.*

admit that some of my challenges as a Christian have been amplified because of the digital readiness of sin. I have often pined for a monastic-like experience that would somehow extricate me from the readiness of temptation.

We are aliens and strangers in this world.[42] The word "alien" gives us one of the best metaphors for our Christian experience. Like the aliens in the relatively new genre of science fiction, we have a similar experience in Christ. We have been inculcated with a spiritual life from another realm. We follow a King from outside of our physical dimension. We take orders from and give our allegiance to this King. We have a new alien force within us that inspires us to live differently from our neighbor.

In addition to this, our allegiance to our King and His alien force within us turns us into a subversive element in this world. We recognize a spiritual influence in this world that promotes a rebellious fallen-ness away from the will and way of the Creator. It has taken the world in directions contrary to the direction God intended for His creation. When we are restored spiritually to the way God intended, we become so different on the inside that we are now considered as aliens to this outside world.

Let me be even more explicit with this alien metaphor. Our alien King has commanded us to go out into this world and spread alien spores.[43] These spores will grow inside of the human recipients and transform them into fellow aliens. We are then to help them shift their allegiance to the alien King from every other allegiance, devotion and authority.[44] These new alien people live by a new and different ethic and force. Everything they do is governed by

---

[42] 1 Peter 2:11 (NIV) *Dear friends, I urge you, as aliens and strangers in the world, to abstain from sinful desires, which war against your soul.*

[43] 1 Peter 1:23 We have been born again by the seed (another word for spore) of the word of God. Being born again means that we are transformed from within.

[44] Luke 14:26-27 (NIV) *If anyone comes to me and does not hate his father and mother, his wife and children, his brothers and sisters—yes, even his own life—he cannot be my disciple. And anyone who does not carry his cross and follow me cannot be my disciple.*

this new force. The new alien force is love,[45] the same kind of love that is at the heart of the very nature of God. Eventually the alien King will come to this planet and establish His reign over all the earth as a benevolent, loving dictator.

With this previous narrative an Amish-type experience doesn't seem that far-fetched. As strange as the last paragraph sounds it really is our story. Because we are aliens from another realm, we must find ways to bridge the gap between our Christian community and the "nations" whom we are called to make disciples of Jesus.

The Context of Discipleship

In the Great Commission Jesus used a word translated "nations" in most versions that loses some of its meaning in translation. The word in the Greek is "ethnos" which has a broader meaning than the way we think of nations today.[46] It means people groups such as tribes, ethnic groupings and sub-cultures. Certainly Bruce Olson's Motilones would be considered an "ethnos," being of a different language and possessing their own set of customs. But "ethnos" cannot be thought of as exclusive to such obvious differences. Paul's statements in 1 Corinthians 9:19-23 shows that he saw the need to identify with the "ethnos" going beyond mere borders and language into the various

---

[45] Galatians 5:14 (NIV) *The entire law is summed up in a single command: "Love your neighbor as yourself."*

[46] IVP New Testament Commentaries on Matthew 28: "*All nations* may signify all groups of "peoples," rather than the modern concept of "nation-states" (McGavran and Arn 1977:38); in many nations a variety of different peoples coexist. Thus Christ commands us to sensitively reach each culture, not merely some people from each nation. Also, far from abandoning the mission to Matthew's own people, his commission represents "peoples" and not simply "Gentiles" (Saldarini 1994:59-60, 78-81; compare Meier 1977), although in the context of his whole Gospel he lays the emphasis on Gentile peoples, whom his community most needs to be encouraged in evangelizing." "The Report of the Church." *BibleGateway.com*. Gospel Communications. 5 April 2006
http://www.biblegateway.com/resources/commentaries/index.php?

sub-cultures of his day. He speaks of economic, religious and moral distinctions: *"to the weak I became weak," "to the Jews I became like a Jew,"* and *"to those not having the law I became like one not having the law."(NIV)*

We are undergoing an "ethnos" transformation in our culture from one generation to the next. Our cultural landscape is changing so fast that our grandchildren will live in a world that has almost no resemblance to the world in which our parents grew up. If the Church is to stay relevant and follow the command of Jesus to *"make disciples of all nations,"*[47] then we must retool, so to speak, in order to both identify with and communicate to the new emerging culture.

The "ethnos" we are specially called to reach determines the context of discipleship. The context determines the methods, language and interactions of the discipleship relationship with that particular "ethnos." Bruce Olson had to employ a very different means to reach the Motilone than we would employ to reach a digital culture. As the Motilone people continued in their path toward discipleship, they sought ways to serve their people and the ethnic groups around them. They sought further means of education and growth for their young people in the medical and engineering sciences. The Gospel so transformed their lives that they saw themselves as agents of the Kingdom of God. They have answered the call to reach those in their "ethnos" group and similar groups in their region.

Because the context of our culture is changing so dramatically we must also consider that the context of our discipleship is changing just as dramatically. In the same way Bruce Olson has given wise and steadfast leadership within his context of discipleship, the Church of the new millennium must provide wise and steadfast leadership to this new digital generation. Bruce Olson inspired the young people of the Motilones to pursue outside education in order to serve in a professional and relevant capacity to their culture and region. We must also inspire and train our young

---

[47] Matthew 28:19 (NIV)

people to find the places of professional and relevant service to our people and region.

Evangelical Christianity continues to be distracted with a shortsighted view of the future. Discipleship has often taken a back seat to eschatology.[48] This has, and continues to keep our vision heavenward rather than on the souls of people suffering in the blight of spiritual darkness in this world. We tend to de-emphasize education and devalue careers that take a lifetime to accomplish a significant impact upon our culture. Dare I say it? We proclaim the imminent return of Christ to the exclusion of developing a long-term strategic plan to reach our culture.

We need to develop these long-term generational plans with the patience and vision of the architects in the Middle Ages. They knew their cathedrals[49] would take so many years to build that they had no hope of seeing them completed in their lifetime. Often these enormous structures would take centuries to complete. If the Church of the Middle Ages can invest so much planning and time to build physical monoliths, could not the Church of our era, the digital age, invest in our youth to reach far into the future of this godless, secular culture?

The context of our "Great Commission" means that we have to invest in and inspire this generation to become digital missionaries. This doesn't necessarily mean that every-thing we do will involve gazing into a computer monitor. What it does mean is that our efforts, training and focus has to move to the relevant fields of growth and change in our culture. We must raise up communication specialists, digital data miners, biotechnical scientists, robotic engineers, and postmodern digital philosophers. We must discern the gargantuan shifts in our world moving us away from nationalism toward a globalized economy and a different form of governance. We need to call forth our prophets

---

[48] "Eschatology simply defined means the study of last things. That is, eschatology is primarily concerned with the final prophetic events mentioned in the Bible." *Welcome.* http://www.eschatology.com: 5 April 2006

[49] Articles about large-scale ecclesiastic architecture can be found at: http://www.zum.de/whkmla/art/hma/cathedrals.html

to peer into the future and give us practical and distinct direction.

The Curriculum of Discipleship

Unlike the context of discipleship the curriculum always stays the same. The curriculum passed down from age to age remains steadfast. No matter where we find ourselves as Christians in the fallen world we have the same mandate. The Motilones must learn the same thing as the digital generation. Simply stated in Jesus' last words: *"...teaching them to obey everything I have commanded you..."*[50]

This unchanging message from the past gives us the necessary anchor that connects us to Christian orthodoxy. It connects us with every Christian of all time in every place and culture. We are all equally commanded to follow the teachings of Jesus and His apostles. I include His apostles because everything Jesus commanded us to live and do comes to us through the writings of these eleven apostles, plus one (that one being Paul).

We are not looking for a new message or a new theology. In fact, most of our work is trying to find out what the original message was all about. Jude put it this way in his letter to the saints: *"...I felt I had to write and urge you to contend for the faith that was once for all entrusted to the saints."*[51] Any movement or message that may seem new in our age is really a re-introduction of the faith that was already delivered to the saints, unless of course it is heretical.

I remember a conversation with an airplane service mechanic as he was training a young apprentice. He was emphatic about how their company had absolutely no interest in innovative thinking when it came to airplane maintenance. He instructed the lad to do everything exactly as he was taught. He was to follow the engineering instruc-

---

[50] Matthew 28:20 (NIV)
[51] Jude 3 (NIV)

tions to the letter. He said, "There is no room for original thought in this line of work; people's lives are at stake."

When it comes to the Gospel message there is no room for original thought; people's lives are at stake! We must labor, with all our effort, to get as close to the original curriculum as possible.

I am not advocating strict legalism here. In fact the curriculum is explicitly against such a position. We are agents of love, not of the law.[52] Love is the prevailing motivation of all we do in the Kingdom of God and love is defined by the personal attributes of God.

It is this curriculum of love for God first, and our fellow man second,[53] that causes us to leave our comfortable traditions and etiquette and venture out into strange territory to reach the "ethnos."

Here is where Paul's instruction to "become all things to all men" finds its connection to the unchanging curriculum. If we are motivated by a sincere love for God and our fellow man then we can adapt without losing our conscience.

When I first came to Christ in the 70s, the big cultural controversy raging among the North American church was the issue of Christian music and rock and roll. I heard several sermons about the evils of contemporary Christian music identifying with the world in their wild pulsating style. It didn't matter that their message was full of gospel truth. We were told that the beat itself was evil and no good thing could come from such a rotten tree.

This whole controversy was settled for me when I was driving with a fellow sailor friend. I had been sharing Christ with this guy and he was very interested in learning more about the gospel. He was a musician and the one thing that held him back was his disdain for church music. Being a drummer, he saw no future for his rock and roll

---

[52] Galatians 5:14 (NIV) *"The entire **law** is summed up in a single command: '**Love** your neighbor as yourself.'"*

[53] Matthew 22:38-40 (NIV) *"This is the first and greatest commandment. And the second is like it: 'Love your neighbor as yourself.' All the Law and the Prophets hang on these two commandments."*

style of play. After several late night discussions, answering a myriad of questions, I finally convinced my buddy to come to church with me. While on the way, I suggested that we listen to some Christian music and he reluctantly consented. I had the latest album on tape from the popular Christian rock group called the "2nd Chapter of Acts."[54]Their opening song started with a hymn-like introduction where their two female singers sounded like angels. I admitted that I too didn't like "churchie" sounding music and apologized. The intro to the song lasted twenty seconds and transitioned abruptly into a rocking guitar solo by Phil Keaggy[55] that rivaled Jimmy Hendricks. The rest of the cassette was filled with excellent rock music exalting Christ. I will never forget the look on my buddy's face when Keaggy amped up the music. He stopped and wondered what was happening. In the next couple of minutes he realized that, not only had I tricked him, but more importantly, his love for a cultural style of music did not create the barrier he imagined. He became a Christian that evening in the church service.

The curriculum remained the same. The words in most of their songs were directly from scripture but the method of bringing the message changed with the culture they were called to reach. We must find every possible means to communicate to and identify with this emerging culture in order to fulfill the Great Commission.

The curriculum has always been about the great narrative of the scriptures. It begins with creation and the fall of man into sin. The centerpiece of the story is the coming of our Lord Jesus Christ in the flesh to identify with mankind and lead him back to God. The revelation of the finished work of Christ through His death, burial and resurrection gives us the foundation of our forgiveness and relationship with God. The understanding of who we are in Christ and all we have in Christ establishes us in our new

---

[54] Check out their history and influence on modern day Christian music at http://www.2ndchapterofacts.com

[55] Phil Keaggy was one of the most significant pioneers in Christian contemporary music. There is a good sampling of his music on this site: http://www.philkeaggy.com

creation identity. The power of the Holy Spirit in our lives and His infilling gives us the power and spiritual strength to live as overcomers in this fallen world and demonstrate the risen majesty of our Lord Jesus.

It is these and other Biblical truths that we are commissioned by Jesus to bring and demonstrate to every culture and sub-culture of our world.

The Means of Discipleship

It is here where the blend of context and curriculum find their practical means. Discipleship is, by its very nature, a relational term. There is one who receives discipleship and one who gives discipleship.

The best metaphor for this relationship is the idea of apprenticeship. Unfortunately the word is getting a bad name because of the recent "reality TV" show featuring Donald Trump and the contest to become his personal apprentice. In so many ways, this show reveals the world's approach toward discipleship. It is all about competition and greed. There are over a million losers in order to achieve one apprentice. This is in complete contrast to the means and spirit of such a noble relationship in Christ. To be a disciple of Jesus means that you will become His apprentice which requires no contest to win this prize of God's grace.

My home church is blessed with a large number of tradesmen. Many of them are participating in the journeyman-apprentice relationship.

Apprenticeship is a highly relational idea. Perhaps the most important aspect of apprenticeship is the relationship between the apprentice and the journeyman. In many cases, the journeyman is the one who recruits the novice. They initiate and give the beginning inspiration for the apprentice to pursue the craft and trade. They give the apprentice their first experiences within the craft and, in most cases, supply their first income in the trade. The journeyman is the first teacher who lays the primary paradigms of understanding about the craft and trade. There is a specific accountability in this relationship but that accountability finds a larger context within the trade.

The journeyman-apprentice relationship is one of instruction, guidance, inspiration, employment and accountability. Consider an electrical apprenticeship. The primary level of accountability comes from the physics of electricity. There are certain things you can and cannot do with electricity. This is the basic curriculum for the apprentice. It determines the entire nature of the craft and ultimately the trade. To overstate the obvious, the journeyman cannot train the apprentice to cause electricity to do things that are physically impossible or dangerous. Understanding the differences of volts and amps, how much power can go through a wire and what materials conduct electricity are the foundational concepts that must be taught and passed on.

The secondary area of curriculum that the apprentice must learn is the specific code within the jurisdiction of the apprenticeship. Every region applies the physics of electricity a bit differently. If you were to do your electrical apprenticeship in Europe where they use a 220-three phase approach, then you would need to learn a different way of applying the physics of electricity. Contrast this with the 120-two phase system you would learn in North America. The physics of electricity don't change because you are in Europe or North America but the application of those physics can and do change. Therefore each jurisdiction has their own way of doing things and this is what makes up the specifics of the "code" for that area.

It is in this application of the "code" that a larger accountability structure is involved with the apprenticeship. The governing jurisdiction has its own way of applying codes and standards for their specific region. Both the apprentice and journeyman find themselves accountable to this larger authority.

In our region (British Columbia) an electrical apprenticeship lasts four years. During this time the apprentice must attend several courses and pass several exams in order to complete their training. This brings a larger sense of accountability into the apprenticeship relationship.

Discipleship and apprenticeship are almost identical terms. Most people come into discipleship through a more experienced Christian. This Christian develops a sense of accountability for their new-found disciple. They begin a process of initiation into the Christian faith. This may involve new believer classes at their local church or one-on-one time laying the foundational paradigms of the Christian faith. It is within this new relationship that the disciple has his new experiences in Christianity. The discipler has the responsibility to interpret and help the disciple through this process.

Like the journeyman-apprentice relationship, the discipleship relationship has a much larger context of accountability. In our example, the first level of accountability is the physics of electricity. In the discipleship relationship this external reality is the Word of Truth. Jesus laid this foundation in John 8:31-32 (KJV): *"Then said Jesus to those Jews which believed on him, If ye continue in my word, then are ye my disciples indeed; And ye shall know the truth, and the truth shall make you free."* I expand this to mean the orthodox teachings of the Christian faith and the broad application of scripture. In a sense, this is the physics of Christianity.

Again, like the journeyman-apprentice relationship, the discipleship relationship has a broader governance. The local church brings to the specific jurisdiction the interpretation and application of the truth. This forms the "code," so to speak, of how this jurisdiction applies the truths of Christianity in its particular culture. Both the discipler and the disciple are accountable to their relationship with this agency.

It continues to be the role of the local church to help its disciples through to the next level of growth and to help supervise their greater relationship within the culture. We are not left to ourselves to determine how, when and where we are to relate to the surrounding culture. We have a heavenly agency to superintend our apprenticeship.

I write to inspire this relationship. Too often people who are innovative in their connection to culture are marginalized and criticized by the church. I refer back to the Christian music debate. It took some time before the church I attended was comfortable with the idea that rock and roll was an acceptable medium for the gospel. In that process many young musicians went through undo pressure and many became disillusioned with the need for any accountability to the church.

We will find ourselves imbedded in the same types of conflict with our digital missionaries if we don't begin to consider ways to disciple and guide them through their call. We need to apply the "code" to some of the very difficult moral, ethical and spiritual battles that await our digital disciples.

This is more than preparing our youth for the work force. It is commissioning them to go into all aspects of our culture and preach the gospel. We must equip them as missionaries to go into the world of communications, science, mathematics, biology, genetics, robotics, nanotechnology, and the many places and professions being transformed by a flattening global world.

Section Two

The Four Digital Transformations

"The World is Flat"

Thomas L. Friedman
Journalist, Author

The Communication Revolution

*"Beneath the rule of men entirely great
The pen is mightier than the sword."*
Edward Bulwer-Lytton[56]

Words command ideas and ideas command empires. Whoever controls the words controls the world. Have you heard the old cliché: "It's not what you know, it's who you know?" Not any more. The power brokers of knowledge are gone. The sages of the ivory towers and the protectors of truth have been reduced to mere mortals. How about a few more clichés: "The cat is out of the bag," because, "there is a new sheriff in town," or more correctly there is NO sheriff in town. The digital world and the internet have dismantled the old authority structures that protected the dissemination of knowledge as their chief source of power over the masses.

A Lesson from Socrates

Socrates, in the ancient writings of Plato, tells the story of Thamus, the King of Egypt, and Theuth, the god of

---

[56] Edward George Earl Bulwer-Lytton, 1st Baron Lytton. *Richelieu, Act II, Scene 2.* English playwright, novelist, & politician (1803 - 1873)

invention. Greek mythology taught that Theuth was the creator of numbers, calculation, astronomy and most importantly, writing. Theuth came to King Thamus explaining that he should allow the Egyptian people to take part in all of his wonderful inventions. Here is part of Plato's narrative taken from "Phaedrus:"

"Thamus inquired into the use of each of them, and as Theuth went through them expressed approval or disapproval, according as he judged Theuth's claims to be well or ill founded. It would take too long to go through all that Thamus is reported to have said for and against each of Theuth's inventions. But when it came to writing, Theuth declared, "Here is an accomplishment, my lord the King, which will improve both the wisdom and the memory of the Egyptians. I have discovered a sure receipt for memory and wisdom." To this, Thamus replied, "Theuth, my paragon of inventors, the discoverer of an art is not the best judge of the good or harm which will accrue to those who practice it. So it is in this; you, who are the father of writing, have out of fondness for your off-spring attributed to it quite the opposite of its real function. Those who acquire it will cease to exercise their memory and become forgetful; they will rely on writing to bring things to their remembrance by external signs instead of by their own internal resources. What you have discovered is a receipt for recollection, not for memory. And as for wisdom, your pupils will have the reputation for it without the reality: they will receive a quantity of information without proper instruction, and in consequence be thought very knowledgeable when they are for the most part quite ignorant. And because they are filled with the conceit of wisdom instead of real wisdom they will be a burden to society."
[57]

---

[57] Plato's *Phaedrus* is a dialogue between Socrates and Phaedrus. The *Phaedrus* was presumably composed around 370 B.C, around the same time as Plato's Republic and Symposium. Although it is primarily about the topic

King Thamus showed great wisdom on his part for his reluctance to receive the invention of writing. Though he was correct about the effects this technology would have on his people's minds, he failed to see an even greater concern to his throne. Writers would become "a burden to society" because they would be able to communicate their thoughts outside of the King's control. Obviously, Thamus also missed the amazing good that such a technology would bring his people. To convey knowledge through written text creates cultural advancement from generation to generation. Thamus failed to see that his people's memory and wisdom were already short-sighted.

The Communication Revolution is upon us. Socrates presents us with an interesting question. Should we accept this "gift?" If we look at it from Thamus' position, I dare say, "we should not; it is too risky; our throne could not withstand such a powerful tool in the hands of the people." But let's remember who we are. Are we not trying to create a subversive element in the world? Is this not an opportunity to topple those who have controlled the thoughts and minds of our culture?

The Church's Earliest Gift of Technology

Around the time of Christ a new technology was emerging. It made its way into everyday culture by the late first century. Up until this point in human history mankind communicated primarily through word of mouth. Anything that needed to be written down for posterity's sake was recorded on scrolls. These rolls of wax tablets and papyrus were very expensive and cumbersome. These scrolls were only found in wealthy schools, libraries, government offices and places of worship. You wouldn't find any form of the

---

of love, the dialogue revolves around a discussion of rhetoric and how it should be practiced. I followed the lead of Neil Postman in *Technopoly*; he uses this story as an example of the written word being one of the earliest technologies to change the basis of culture.

written word in the homes of the common man, until the Codex.[58] This new type of "information technology" had dramatic effects on the distribution of the scriptures in the early centuries of the church. Instead of hauling carts of scrolls, a person could simply bind it in a single book. The Codex was the first real book made of paper-thin animal skins and could be written on both sides of the parchment.

Historians, archeologists and especially textual critics[59] are blessed with an amazing abundance of manuscript evidence of the Old and New Testaments from this period. The plethora of evidence exists because the early church adopted this new technology of the Codex. It became the primary means of distributing the Word of God. By the second century there were copies of the scriptures in nearly every house church.

Today there are 5,686 extant copies of the Greek New Testament dating from the second to the sixth century. There are only hundreds of copies of some of the most important books of that era or earlier; such as Homer's Illiad, 643; Sophocles, 193; and our beloved Plato quoted earlier, 7. In addition, there are over 19,000 copies of the New Testament in the Syriac, Latin, Coptic and Aramaic languages bringing the total manuscript base to over 24,000 copies.[60]

---

[58] Codex. Wikipedia, The Free Encyclopedia. 5 April 2006 23:19 UTC http://en.wikipedia.org/wiki/Codex "A codex (Latin for book; plural codices) is a handwritten book from late Antiquity or the Early Middle Ages. Although the Romans used the codex and similar precursors made of wood for taking notes and other informal writings, the first recorded use of the codex for literary works dates from the late first century, when Martial experimented with the format. At that time, the roll (also called a scroll) was the dominant medium for literary works and would remain dominant for secular works until the 4th century. As far back as the early 2nd century, there is evidence that the codex was the preferred format among Christians, while other religions preferred the roll. The Christian codex was made of papyrus, more compact and better suited for people on the move than parchment."

[59] Textual Critics are those who are dedicate to the science of manuscripts and to finding the most accurate extant copies that are closest to the original.

[60] This data is well known among archaeologists and Greek specialists of this era. I first discovered this from reading Josh McDowell's *Evidence that*

The young church was able to embrace and adapt to this new way of communication. Other religions, including Judaism, had too much invested in the older communication media. In some cases the scrolls themselves became holy relics. To change these would be sacrilegious. The new and upcoming Christian movement on the other hand, had no specific allegiance to the older medium. It was ready for the "new wine skin"[61] of the codex and eventually changed the entire Roman world with it!

We All Want to Change the World

In 1370, an English scholar emerged with a vision to change Europe forever. This scholar wanted the same thing the internet has done. He wanted to get information to the masses that would enable them to make their own decisions regarding truth. This would give them the ability to touch the face of God without holding the hand of the educated priest.

His name was John Wycliffe[62] and he was the first to translate the Bible from Latin into English. Perhaps his most famous statement was, "I believe that in the end truth will conquer." His notoriety and scholarship was renown throughout all of Europe. His writings had a wide circulation and became the foundation for a pre-reformation to

---

Demands a Verdict as an early Christian. It forever settled the criticism that the Scriptures are some contrived book written by a monk in the middle ages. This is vital information for young believers of our day who have to do battle with such fallacies as recently presented in the popular book and movie *The DaVinci Code*.
http://www.carm.org/evidence/textualevidence.htm

[61] Matthew 9:17 (NIV) *"Neither do men pour new wine into old wineskins. If they do, the skins will burst, the wine will run out and the wineskins will be ruined. No, they pour new wine into new wineskins, and both are preserved."*

[62] To learn more about this great Christian leader and scholar go to http://chi.gospelcom.net/GLIMPSEF/Glimpses/glmps013.shtml and http://www.christianitytoday.com/history/special/131christians/wycliffe.html

take place as far away as Bohemia (modern day Austria/Hungry).

The Christian History Institute writes:

> "Wycliffe cared deeply for the poor and common folk and railed against the abuses of the Church. The Church owned over one-third of the land in England. Clergy were often illiterate and immoral. High offices in the church were bought or given out as political plums. But the problems went even deeper. Wycliffe, a devoted student of the Bible, saw that some of the doctrines of the church had departed from biblical moorings. Based on his study of the Scripture, he wrote and preached against the teachings about purgatory, the sale of indulgences, and the doctrine of transubstantiation."

Wycliffe not only stepped on the religious toes of the Roman Catholic Church but also the power structures of European politics. He declared, "This Bible is for the government of the people, by the people and for the people."[63] He saw correctly that if the control of knowledge (in this case the Bible) could be given to the people then they would begin to challenge the powers that be and bring change. Unfortunately, Wycliffe was removed from his post as Chief Scholar of Oxford University and banished from preaching. He went to work on his translation of the scriptures which his followers would faithfully copy and distribute throughout England. His translations where confiscated and his followers were burned at the stake. The classic, *Foxes Book of Martyrs* by John Foxe, focuses much of its attention on the enormous sacrifices of these people.

---

[63] *John Wycliffe quotes*. ThinkExist.com Quotations. 1 Mar. 2006. http://10.1.0.25/quotes/john_wycliffe This phrase is found in the introduction to his translation of the Bible in 1382. Originally, Wycliffe meant this to apply only to church government but it wasn't long before this idea was conveyed in civil government as well. It is likely that Abraham Lincoln found his inspiration from Wycliffe when he used almost identical language in the Gettysburg Address.

What did Wycliffe lack? Why is he only know as the "Morning Star of the Reformation" and not the Father thereof, the title given to Martin Luther? Simply stated it was the Gutenberg printing press. Some historians would argue that Wycliffe would have made a better leader of the Reformation. His theology was far more temperate and it presented a strong balanced understanding of the role of the state. Regardless of this, Wycliffe's time lacked the technology to mass produce his message and thus the religious and political authorities in his day successfully muffled his message and held the reformation back for another 150 years.

Moveable Type - The Catalyst for World Change

Somewhere in the poorer section of Mainz around 1400, Johann Gutenberg[64] was born. His father was a blacksmith who specialized in minting gold coins. Johann would inherit the family trade but he would never shake his inclination toward invention.

Johann later moved to Strasburg where his family had stronger political connections. It was here that he found acceptance in the goldsmiths' guild. It was in the company of such a highly technical group of men that he gained the knowledge and resources to begin his invention. Johann became one of the primary managers and technicians in the guild. It is here, undoubtedly, that he came across some of the challenges of printing. Printing was a very expensive process. Large metal plates were forged or wooden plates were carved to print a single page.

Johann's idea was simple, if he could forge or carve each letter separately, and in enough abundance, he could reuse the type for various different print jobs. As he set out to build the press, he began to face serious personal problems. In 1437 he was sued for "breach of promise of mar-

---

[64] Most of my biographical information about Gutenberg can be found in the Catholic Encyclopedia located at:
http://www.newadvent.org/cathen/07090a.htm

riage" by a young patrician girl. This failed betrothal eventually meant that Johann had to leave Strasburg and return to Mainz, leaving him penniless and unable to complete the final aspects of his project.

Gutenberg literally lived off the generosity of his extended family in order to keep working on the press. In 1450, he formed a partnership with Johann Fust and was able to put the finishing touches on his invention. With Fust's backing Johann launched into the ambitious first print job – the "42-lined" printed version of the Latin Vulgate Bible.[65] This project took Johann nearly five years to complete which went well beyond the patience of his financial patron. When the project was finished Fust sued Johann and successfully obtained ownership of the press and all that had been printed to that date. Two years later Johann had to surrender the founts of type which he had developed two decades earlier. He died penniless ten years later as a ward of the church.

Johann Gutenberg had a vision of an effective way to communicate more efficiently. Like any inventor he was devoted to his creative idea. There is no doubt that he was also a faithful adherent to the Christianity of his day. He had no idea that his work would change the world and be

---

[65] *Gutenberg Bible* Wikipedia, The Free Encyclopedia. 29 March 2006 02:25 UTC http://en.wikipedia.org/wiki/Gutenberg_Bible "The Gutenberg Bible (also known as the 42-line Bible, and as the Mazarin Bible) is a print of the Latin Vulgate translation of the Bible that was printed by its namesake, Johann Gutenberg, in Mainz, Germany. The print run started on February 23, 1455, using moveable type. This Bible is the most famous incunabulum and its production marked the beginning of the mass production of books in the West. ... A very complete copy comprises 1282 pages; most were bound in two volumes.

"It is believed that about 180 copies of the Bible were produced, 45 on vellum and 135 on paper, a number which boggled minds in societies which, from time immemorial, had to produce copies of written works laboriously by hand. Gutenberg produced these Bibles (which were printed, then rubricated and illuminated by hand), over a period of three years, the time it would have taken to produce one copy in a Scriptorium. Because of the hand illumination, each copy is unique. Two-color printing techniques, which would have eliminated the need for rubrication, were developed later."

considered the most important invention of the millennium. We can only speculate, had he foreseen the events which were about to tear his political and spiritual world apart, that he may not have devoted his life to such a dangerous instrument of change.

Thamus' words could easily be spoken to Gutenberg: "Theuth, my paragon of inventors, the discoverer of an art is not the best judge of the good or harm which will accrue to those who practice it. So it is in this; you, who are the father of writing, have out of fondness for your off-spring attributed to it quite the opposite of its real function." These words could also be spoken to today's communication technology inventors. Do they have the foresight to know what their "off-spring" will bring to our world?

The Reformation

Gutenberg's invention, like Theuth's gift of writing, was not the actual instrument of change. But history teaches that any change in communication technology will facilitate a dramatic shift within the culture it is introduced. The technology itself is neutral but those who discover its value are not. The established order or authorities are always late in their discovery of the new technology. Nearly all bureaucracies are established to conserve the status-quo and are not able to handle change well.

The story of Gutenberg's new technology would be incomplete without Martin Luther but the invention's effects were not, in any way, limited to Luther's reformation. No doubt, the Renaissance[66] period of European history owes much of its cultural change to the printing press. The word "renaissance" comes from the Italian word "rinascita,"

---

[66] *Renaissance.* Wikipedia, The Free Encyclopedia. 5 April 2006 18:50 UTC http://en.wikipedia.org/wiki/Renaissance "In the traditional view, the Renaissance is understood as an historical age that was preceded by the Middle Ages and followed by the Reformation. ... A rebirth of classical learning and knowledge through the rediscovery of ancient texts, and also a rebirth of European culture in general."

meaning rebirth. Though scholars argue about when, where and how the Renaissance started, they all agree that it is a "rebirth" of ancient classical ideas. This rebirth of classical learning and knowledge saw a broad distribution because of Gutenberg's invention. By Luther's day fellow contemporary scholars such as Erasmus and Ekk, became notable experts of classical literature.

No historian, secular or religious, will discount Martin Luther's[67] enormous contribution in reforming both the Church and western culture. These changes would have only been a minor theological skirmish in a distant German region without Gutenberg's press.

Martin was a serous child brought up in a strict German home. His mother, who had many children to look after, was a harsh disciplinarian. Martin's father was both a farmer and a miner and later became a very successful merchant. His father did well enough financially to send Martin to the University of Erfurt in the hope that he would become a lawyer. Martin received his first degree in Liberal Arts in 1502 and his Master's degree three years later.

On the way home from his studies he was caught in a lightening storm. Frightened for his eternal soul he cried out to St. Anne for help. He would devote himself to Christian service as a monk if she would spare his life! To his father's disgust and anger, Luther honored this solemn promise and joined the Augustinian order at the Black Monastery in Erfurt.

In 1507, Luther was ordained a priest and began rigorous studies in theology, returning again to the University of Erfurt. During his studies he came into contact with

---

[67] There are so many resources on the life of Martin Luther, his teachings and his movement that anyone interested in his life can find adequate material just about anywhere. I would recommend starting with the recent movie produced by New Look Media, distributed by MGM, staring Joseph Fiennes entitled: "Luther."(2003) The subtitle reads, "One man's faith in God launched the greatest revolution of all." I found the website http://www.luther.de/en/ to be one of the most helpful websites in my research for this book.

the ideas of the Humanists, whose principle spokesperson was Erasmus, and embraced their slogan "Ad Fontes!" – "Back to the Source!" For Luther this meant the study of the Bible in its original Hebrew and Greek languages.

Throughout the next decade of studies Luther became very disillusioned with the Catholic Church. He found himself at odds with his strict conscience and in desperate need for a sense of forgiveness. At one point he was sent to Rome on an errand for his monastery and used the trip to find his assurance in the great Christian city. What he found was a church system misguiding its followers with the false assurance of relics, rituals and indulgences.

He returned to "the source" in his studies: the scriptures and in 1512 became a doctor of theology. Shortly after this he was appointed as the professor of theology at Wittenberg University and installed as the priest over the city's church. Luther began to question the teachings and practices of the Roman Church while he developed much of his reformation theology. Most notably, he began to understand that salvation and forgiveness are the free gift of God through faith in Jesus Christ. He saw and began to teach that no church, Pope or indulgence could add to or take from this reality in the life of the Christian.

In 1517, Pope Leo allowed the regional Archbishop to sell indulgences through the services of the Dominican monk, Johann Tetzel. The practice of buying indulgences[68] replaced the need for confession and repentance. The purchasers of an indulgence would receive forgiveness for their sins, avoid purgatory and help their loved ones escape eter-

---

[68] This definition is found in the official Catholic Catechism: "What is an indulgence? An indulgence is a remission before God of the temporal punishment due to sins whose guilt has already been forgiven, which the faithful Christian who is duly disposed gains under certain prescribed conditions through the action of the Church which, as the minister of redemption, dispenses and applies with authority the treasury of the satisfactions of Christ and the saints. An indulgence is partial or plenary according as it removes either part or all of the temporal punishment due to sin. The faithful can gain indulgences for themselves or apply them to the dead." *Catechism of the Catholic Church - The sacrament of penance and reconciliation.* 5 April 2006. http://www.vatican.va/archive/catechism/p2s2c2a4.htm#X

nal judgment. When some of Luther's congregation returned with indulgences in hand, he was enraged.

Luther had preached against this practice for years but now it had come to his hometown. He responded by writing a letter of protest, giving 95 Thesis[69] (reasons) why the sale of indulgences was not an acceptable Christian practice. On October 31st, he posted this letter on the church door in Wittenberg - a standard practice in this university town to begin discussion and debate on an issue.

Unknown to Luther, in the next few weeks, his 95 Thesis was distributed throughout the region. That night or the next day, two of Luther's congregants took the document to a local printer. There they translated it from Latin to German and printed thousands of copies. In a short time all of Europe was aflame with the controversy. Thus began the Protestant Reformation.

Luther saw the tremendous impact of this technology. He began to print and distribute his remarkable teachings. For the next three years his teachings found the widest distribution of any author to date. Obviously, the Catholic Church had to act. On June 15th, 1520, Luther was officially told to recant his teachings through a Papal Bull of excommunication. Luther reacted in protest by burning the document which resulted in his complete excommunication by the Pope on January 3, 1521.

The Holy Roman Emperor, the King of Spain, gave Luther one more chance to recant his teachings at the Imperial Diet of Worms on April 2nd, 1521. Luther took this as an opportunity to defend his position. Instead he was asked, before the Emperor, to recant all of his teachings. He had to appear before the Emperor twice; each time he was clearly told to take back his teachings. Luther did not see any proof against his theses or views which would move him to recant:

"Unless I am convinced by Scripture and plain reason - I do not accept the authority of the popes and coun-

---

[69] The actual letter is reproduced online at:
http://www.luther.de/en/95thesen.html

cils, for they have contradicted each other - my conscience is captive to the Word of God. I cannot and I will not recant anything, for to go against conscience is neither right nor safe. God help me. Amen. Here I stand. I cannot do otherwise."[70]

At the Diet, a conspiracy was plotted to have Luther killed on his return home. He had traveled to Worms under the protection of his patron and powerful sovereign, Elector Friedrich the Wise of Saxon. Prince Friedrich caught news of this plan and intervened by having Luther whisked away by his own soldiers. He was taken to Friedrich's castle in Wartburg where Luther was exiled for almost a year. The rest of Europe thought Luther to be dead.

While in exile Luther undertook the work of Bible translation. In this short time he translated the New Testament and much of the Old. He sought to bring the scripture to the people. His work was the first translation into a common language to be mass produced. Again the printing press became the primary agent for such prolific change. The Scriptures were now in the hands of the common man. It would only be a short fifteen years until another disciple of Luther, William Tyndale would translate the New Testament into English to be printed and distributed to all of England.

The Modern Gutenberg-ian Invention

"Those who don't know history are destined to repeat it," Edmund Burke.[71]

---

[70] *Luther at the Imperial Diet of Worms (1521)*. KDG Wittenberg. 5 April 2006. http://www.luther.de/en/worms.html Some sources omit the last statement, "Here I stand. I cannot do otherwise."
[71] *Edmund Burke quotes*. ThinkExist.com Quotations Online. 1 March 2006. http://10.1.0.25/quotes/edmund_burke "British statesman, parliamentary orator, and political thinker prominent in public life from 1765 to about 1795 and important in the history of political theory. He championed conservatism in opposition to Jacobinism in *Reflections on the Revolution in*

I have taken us back into the past so that we might peer into the future. The recent advent of the internet and all of the amazing innovations of communication technology in the last fifteen years will prove to surpass Gutenberg's scope of change. If the movable type press released a reformation of change, the internet will unleash a full out revolution. The printing press was accessible only to specific skilled workers; the internet is open to any who can read and write. The printing press was limited to those who could afford to pay to publish; the internet can be accessed for free in most cities around the world. The printing press was only found in the major metropolises of Europe; the internet is now touching every inch of the globe. Hold on mom and dad, we are in for a wild ride!

I heard a student say once, "The internet must have started in outer space." They were partly right. In 1957 the USSR launched "Sputnik" and the world watched as the "evil empire"[72] flew overhead. The U.S. was stunned. How did the Russians beat us to outer-space? It was time to wake up. The U.S. formed the Advanced Research Projects Agency (ARPA) the following year. This well funded, and at the time secret, agency was given the mandate to establish the U.S. as the world leader in every science and technology field applicable to the military.[73]

In order to take the lead, the U.S. saw its opportunity through the advanced computer systems they had started to use in the Department of Defense. But these large mainframe systems lacked the ability to effectively speak to each other. They were hindered by long distances

---

France (1790)." *Edmund Burke.* Britannica Online. 5 April 2006
http://www.britannica.com/eb/article-9018168

[72] This term for the Soviet Union was coined by President Ronald Reagan in 1982 at the 41st Annual Convention of the National Association of Evangelicals. It would spark worldwide debate and eventually lead to meetings between Reagan and the last Soviet Leader Mikhail Gorbachev. The Cold War ended 6 years after Regan's remark.

[73] I consulted several websites in my research of the history of the internet: Two of the most helpful were:
http://www.zakon.org/robert/internet/timeline/ and
http://en.wikipedia.org/wiki/History_of_the_internet

and different computer protocol languages in the various systems. By working together with specific universities, notably MIT, Stanford and UCLA, the network for these computers, ARPANET, was launched at almost the same time as Neil Armstrong set foot on the surface of the moon.

Because ARPA worked extensively with universities, both the Department of Defense and multiple academic institutions began to take advantage of this nation-wide network. By 1971, twenty-three hosts were using the ARPANET. During the next ten years the standard protocols were worked out so that the network could grow. The main network language TCP/IP[74] was decided upon which is the language of the internet today. Programmers using this protocol could now develop applications that would use the network for specific tasks. The first dynamic application to be developed was email. More and more the ARPANET found civilian uses through the connection of universities. Professors in any of the linked institutions now had a way to share data. In 1982, the Norwegians left the European network initiative to adopt the TCP/IP protocol so that they could communicate with American Universities - hinting to the global possibilities of the network. By 1984 there were over 1000 hosts and the network took on a life of its own. The U.S. National Science Foundation began independent research on how to make the ARPANET more stable after the first virus brought the entire network to a halt. When these two projects finally merged, the new name of the network became "the Internet."

The developing European network, called CERNET, started converting their systems to the TCP/IP protocol. By the end of the decade these networks were all linked and the number of hosts jumped to 100,000.

---

[74]*Internet protocol suite.* Wikipedia, The Free Encyclopedia. 4 April 2006 02:38 UTC http://en.wikipedia.org/wiki/TCP/IP "The internet protocol suite is the set of communications protocols that implement the protocol stack on which the Internet and most commercial networks run. It is sometimes called the TCP/IP protocol suite, after the two most important protocols in it: the Transmission Control Protocol (TCP) and the Internet Protocol (IP), which were also the first two defined."

1989 was a crucial turning point for the Internet. Commercial interest was growing and the first non-government, non-academic ISP (Internet Service Provider) was allowed in by the U.S. Government. The universities protested this inclusion but the cost of the infrastructure was becoming a factor in creating more providers. This change in policy also facilitated the creation of several new agencies to manage the Internet. By 1990, ARPANET ceased to exist and the world came online through world.std.com.

At this time users of the internet were struggling to find user-friendly ways to organize and distribute the data. Computer programmer, Tim Berners-Lee, had been working on the concept of hypertext[75] to facilitate sharing and updating of data. By creating a protocol for pages to reveal data rather than just complex directories, Berners-Lee created the World Wide Web (WWW). By making this language available to everyone he created the standard HTTP (HyperText Transfer Protocol) for web page development.

The internet still lacked one crucial application: a way to effectively view this new HTTP format. The application known as Gopher could read hypertext but was unable to organize it into anything except a menu. The High-Performance Computing and Communications Initiative introduced by Senator Al Gore[76] provided research money to develop a graphical browser for the WWW. Marc Andreessen, a junior engineer working for the agency, was respon-

---

[75]*Hypertext.* Wikipedia, The Free Encyclopedia. 5 April 2006 03:03 UTC http://en.wikipedia.org/wiki/Hypertext "In computing, hypertext is a user interface paradigm for displaying documents which, according to an early definition (Nelson 1970), "branch or perform on request." The most frequently discussed form of hypertext document contains automated cross-references to other documents called hyperlinks. Selecting a hyperlink causes the computer to display the linked document within a very short period of time."

[76] Al Gore had to find his way into this book because of his claim that he *helped to invent the internet*, made in his failed attempt for the presidency during the 2000 election campaign against George Bush. *Transcript: Vice President Gore on CNN's 'Late Edition.'* CNN.com. 9 March 1999 17:06 EST

sible to develop this project called Mosaic. This new piece of technology gave the user the ability to view text and graphics in the same format as a printed page. After graduating from university, Andreessen helped form Netscape Communications and named their new invention, Netscape Navigator. In 1994, they posted a beta version of the browser on the web as a free download and the World Wide Web was transformed.

Jim Barksdale, the former CEO of Netscape, in an interview with author and journalist Tom Friedman, commented about the launch of Netscape.

"We put up the Netscape browser,... and people were downloading it for three-month trials. I've never seen volume like this. For big businesses and government it was allowing them to connect and unlock all their information, and the point-and-click system that Marc Andreessen invented allowed mere mortals to use it, not just scientists. And that made it a true revolution. And we said, 'This thing will just grow and grow and grow.'"[77]

When Netscape went public the next year, they leapt onto the scene as the first viable internet company. This started a five year trend of enormous investment in internet technology. All you had to say in an investors meeting was, "I have a dot.com business," and they would literally throw money at you. Barksdale continues:

"We were profitable almost from the start... Netscape was not a dot-com. We did not participate in the dot-com bubble. We *started* the dot-com bubble."[78]

This period of unprecedented investment in such a new technology caused the internet to explode beyond any-

---

[77] Thomas L. Friedman. *The World is Flat.* Farrar, Straus and Giroux, 2005. Page 60. Jim Barksdale, the former CEO of Netscape is quoted from an interview with author.
[78] Ibid., Page 64.

one's wildest predictions. At the beginning of the new millennium, the dot-com bubble began to deflate because of over-investment and, in the wake of the 9/11 terrorist attacks, the bubble burst. But what this period of investment did accomplish was a truly global network: the seamless infrastructure of servers and fiber optics that have given us the internet we use today in virtually every corner of the globe. The internet is here and the world has changed.

The New Language of Communication

The internet is now a mixture of new technologies built on the back of the TCP/IP infrastructure. You might confuse all the names with alphabet soup: HTTP, HTML, FTP, SSL, SMTP, POP3, PHP, etc. These new technologies are enabling us to communicate in ways that were unimaginable just thirty years ago.

Growing up, one of my favorite Saturday morning cartoons was the *Jetsons*. This wonderful sci-fi rendition of our future inspired hours of imagining what the world would be like in hundreds of years with video telephones and flying cars. Today my kids enjoy a video connection with their friends over MSN. I use the new VOIP[79] application called Skype to make computer to computer phone calls. The future came awfully fast. I am waiting to bid on Ebay, in the next few years, for my flying car.

These new applications have turned the internet into the central place for any distance communication. It is only a matter of time and bandwidth before nearly every form of transmission into our homes, schools and offices comes through this portal. The idea of cyberspace is no longer a science fiction fantasy. Cyberspace is becoming the preferred place to meet with our family, friends, students, employees, customers and governments.

Flash and Video technologies are likely to grow faster and bigger than text technology in the next couple of

---

[79] VOIP stands for Voice Over Internet Protocol – some analysts believe it may finally undo century old communication giants such as ATT and Bell.

years. Consider that the single fastest growing industry on the net has been pornography. There are hundreds of thousands of pornographic videos available online for a nominal fee. Both good and evil uses are driving the growth of the internet.

The internet is in the process of changing the new "main street" of our towns and cities. Our North American cities went through major restructuring as business and commerce moved from downtown locations to the suburbs. The new place of commerce and communication will do the same. The most important address to obtain when a new business or product is launched is online. What will your URL (Universal Resource Locator) be? URLs are also called domain names. Imagine how important it is for a company like Sears to own www.sears.com. When I first signed on to the internet in early 1995, I caught a glimpse of how important this might be for our church so I registered www.kcc.net. I had missed www.kcc.com by a few weeks. There are no more three letter dot-com names available from the public registry.

During the dot-com era, certain entrepreneurs foresaw this new cyberspace real estate boom and purchased hundreds of key names. They then auctioned these names off to the highest bidder. Some names sold for millions of dollars. It was like buying up prime real estate in the center of Manhattan. It is believed that www.business.com was the most expensive deal ever selling for $7.5 million dollars! This rate has slowed down in recent years but sales continue to push into the millions of dollars for this prime communication real estate. In July of 2004, a small Austin Texas marketing firm paid $2.75 million for www.creditcards.com. The company's CEO said, "It's like prime real estate, there's only so much of this real estate to go around. I feel like we bought a slice of Park Avenue."[80]

One of the newest phenomenons of the internet is the advent of the "Blog." Hugh Hewitt, conservative politi-

---

[80] Bob Sullivan. *Domain name sells for $2.75 million CreditCards.com deal sparks talk of new gold rush.* MSNBC. 20 July 2004 20:30 ET
http://www.msnbc.msn.com/id/5467584

cal radio analyst and Christian, writes in his book by the same name:

> "...millions of people are changing their habits when it comes to information acquisition. This has happened many times before with the appearance of the printing press, then the telegraph, then the telephone, radio, television and internet. Now, however, the blogosphere has appeared and it has come so suddenly as to surprise even the most sophisticated of analysts. My WordPerfect 11 software doesn't even recognize the word blogosphere, as I discovered on my return flight from New York to California on the Saturday after the Republican National Convention in early September 2004 where a few dozen bloggers provided yet more evidence of the revolution underway in information acquisition. Technorati (www.technorati.com), a must-used tool in navigation in the blogosphere, counts more than 4 million blogs in being as 2004 came to a close. That's a pretty big thing to miss for the folks over at WordPerfect. But lots of people are missing the blogs."[81]

The word "blog" comes from "Web log." This is a website where the author or authors post regular, time-dated material. These posts can be anything from political commentary as in www.hughhewitt.com to the periodical thoughts and ramblings of a youth pastor, like our school Chaplin, Dan Knorr, at: http://www.xanga.com/dman_0911. Blogging has become the quickest and easiest way to get your thoughts online. At the date of this writing, Technorati lists 31.1 million blogs on its search list. Keep in mind that this number includes blogs that haven't been updated in the last year, a fate that comes to half of the blogs posted. Those blogs that are renewed periodically seem to develop a

---

[81] Hugh Hewitt. *Blog*. Oasis Audio, 2004. Introduction Time 00:02:42. I downloaded this book through www.audible.com. You can visit Hewitt's blog site at: http://www.hughhewlett.com.

life of their own. As I write this, Boing Boing[82] is the most popular blog in the world. In January 2006, it had over two and a half million visitors to the site. This is an advertiser's paradise. The average blogger is still a teenage girl but this is changing in the blogosphere.

Blogs are becoming a preferred media outlet for those who are tired of print and broadcast media. Hewitt's book points to the dramatic effect that bloggers had in the 2004 presidential election campaign. It was bloggers that unveiled false statements given by John Kerry concerning his military service record in Cambodia during the late 60's. It was bloggers that vindicated George Bush when CBS anchorman, Dan Rather, presented falsified documents of disciplinary action in Bush's service record. Hewitt coined the phrase blog-swarm: when a person, business or organization comes under the scrutiny and attack of the blogosphere. Because bloggers link to each other and pass on communication as fast as they can cut and paste, they have begun to have immediate and direct impact upon how a news story is told.

In our church staff meeting, our men's group leader mentioned that we should consider starting an email newsletter for the men of the Church. I suggested that he start a blog. As I made this suggestion half of the staff at the meeting had no idea what a blog was. I remarked that many of their own children were bloggers who were already published authors and poets. The men's ministry leader gave a smirk but his expression changed when I showed him and the staff his fifteen-year-old daughter's web page where she frequently blogs her thoughts and feelings. He was astonished that his daughter was an accomplished and published writer and that people frequently visited her site.

I doubt that blogging will ever usurp the place of email on the net. Regardless of what internet "medium" is

---

[82]http://www.boingboing.net/ Boing Boing is a weblog of cultural curiosities and interesting technologies. It's the most popular blog in the world, as ranked by Technorati.com, and won the Lifetime Achievement and Best Group Blog awards at the 2006 Bloggies ceremony. It is very liberal in its ideas. It also advertises for pornographic sites, so beware.

used, it is clear that the pre-internet days can be thought of as the old world and post-internet days as the new world.

Communication Disciples

In early 2004 we began the start-up process of Heritage Christian Online School.[83] We saw this as a great opportunity to extend our arms of discipleship beyond our geographical borders. When I presented the plan to our board, I said we would consider it a successful start if 100 students enrolled. We began our first year with 430 students. In our second year, we grew to 750 students that made us the largest online, evangelical Christian school in Canada. We have also started online delivery of courses to other Christian schools. We have a team of 45 teachers around the province of British Columbia.

We have begun to disciple online. It is not the easiest way to educate. It isn't always the most enjoyable way to educate. What we have learned is that when the parent stays involved, as in a traditional campus school, the students will succeed. Some things will never change.

The real story of the Online School is how we built it. For the last fifteen years I have emphasized the need to stay technically current at Heritage Christian School.[84] We have never had huge financial resources available but we always maintained a good computer lab and program. In the last few years, we taught and emphasized web based development. From our student body we had several students excel in website design and one student in particular began his career in computer engineering while still in high school.

---

[83] http://www.onlineschool.ca is the Heritage Christian Online School website. We also have launched http://www.bconlineschools.ca to bring online courses to other schools. In April 2006, we launched one of BC's largest home school conventions – http://www.bcconvention.ca .

[84] http://www.heritagechristian.ca This is our campus, Grades K to 12 program.

With this homegrown pool of talent, we had a ready made, low cost, Christian work force available to take on the huge task of building an online K-12 school. We commissioned teachers to write the courses in a simple MS Word format. Our "Enhancement Team," as we call them, reformatted the content, added graphics, video, java scripts, etc. Steven, our engineer wrote an amazing online data base for our teachers and families so that the students could enroll, register for courses, track their progress based on Provincial outcomes and get report cards online. For us older folk the learning curve was steep but for these young adults it was as if they were in their natural habitat.

The point of this section is not to direct everyone to start online discipleship programs. Yes, the internet gives us a much broader potential to break out of our geographical limitations. Yes, the church and the Christian school movement need to learn how to do this. But more importantly, the point is that our community began to make communication disciples. A big part of our immediate success can be attributed to the team of dedicated Christian young people who received specific training in this field.

Once these skills are grown and developed, the entire world will open up to those with the vision to exploit these talents.

As I am writing the final pages of this book, my friend and colleague in Christian schooling, Pat Hayden, is pursing a new vision. Pat grew up believing that most Christians are unthinking air-heads. In his search for truth, he despised the way many Christians gave him simplistic answers to his tough questions. Pat became a Christian and eventually sold everything to pursue his dreams of missions and education. He is the science teacher for Heritage Christian School and wrote most of the science courses for Heritage Christian Online School.

Pat is working on a project that will help youth across Canada connect around the serious moral issues facing our country. *Young Minds for Canada,* or www.ym4c.ca, will give Christian and conservatively minded young people a chance to collectively discuss hard topics such as same sex marriage, the age of sexual consent, abortion, euthanasia, health care, etc. His goal is to give these youth a clarion voice to our nation. The best of these discussions in the forums and blogs will be published and personally distributed to our politicians and cultural leaders. The digital ability to communicate will allow one man to gather a Gideon-like[85] army and answer the call of God to nurture young minds. Margaret Mead is quoted on the ym4c.ca website:

"Never doubt that a small group of thoughtful, committed citizens can change the world. Indeed, it is the only thing that ever has."[86]

The Christian home, school and church must take the responsibility to grow and develop communication disciples. Too often we leave the specifics of the technical training to secular institutions. The current strategy is to raise strong, Christian young people and when they are ready, send them to secular institutions for training. This approach facilitates a dualistic mentality toward their faith and their work. Our young people often imbibe worldviews specific to their field that often don't fit within their Christian calling. The Christian community needs to develop strategies for developing our youth as communication specialists. Communication technology training should be compulsory in the same way as any other core subject in our high schools.

---

[85] Judges 7:1-7. This interesting story shows how God scaled down Gideon's army to those who were watchful. After the weak and fearful were dismissed, Gideon is instructed to take only those solders who do not drink with their faces in the water but stoop down and drink by cupping their hands. In this way the solders were able to see all around and maintain an alert posture.

[86] A www.ym4c.ca rotating quote. "Margaret Mead (December 16, 1901 – November 15, 1978) was an American cultural anthropologist." *Margaret Mead*. Wikipedia, The Free Encyclopedia. 5 April 2006 01:52 UTC http://en.wikipedia.org/wiki/Margaret_Mead

Online Accountability

Discipleship means a relationship with accountability. The new landscape of internet communication is fraught with dangers. We are foolish if we think we are immune to these dangers because we are Christians. The temptation of pornography on the internet is unavoidable. Thankfully there is technology that will help. Content filtering[87] is a must for most men and some women. Parents, educators and employers must educate themselves in how to lock out the smut on our computers lest we raise a generation of sex addicts. Each home, school and workplace should develop a strict policy[88] on how to handle this danger. If we are going to advance in this new genre we must work hard to avoid as much temptation as possible.

Another frequent danger is the temptation of anonymity. People online are not always what they seem. We teach our children to avoid strangers in the outside world but they can meet all manner of strangers online. They will encounter people online that they have never met and have no idea who they really are. This poses obvious dangers for our children but it is also tempting to pass ourselves off as someone we are not. How many of us have logged on to someone else's computer and used their MSN Messenger profile? You don't always know who you are talking to online.

The answer for these and other online temptations is accountability. We must allow transparent and accountable relationships into our lives. The Apostle Paul exhorted us in 2 Corinthians 4:2:

---

[87] A simple Google search of "Content Filter reviews" will present several good options. In my home we are now using ContentProtect found at: http://www.contentwatch.com/ We have also used Cybersitter successfully for many years it can be found at: http://www.cybersitter.com

[88] In my home my wife has maintained the password so that I avoid the temptation as well. She receives an email when potential sites are blocked. I also have a close friend with whom I communicate regularly on this issue.

We refuse to wear masks and play games. We don't maneuver and manipulate behind the scenes. And we don't twist God's Word to suit ourselves. Rather, we keep everything we do and say out in the open, the whole truth on display, so that those who want to can see and judge for themselves in the presence of God.
(The Message)

Any and all true spiritual power will come from a life of open, transparent honesty and truth.

Our accountability must go beyond the things we should prevent and include the things we should be doing. I am always surprised when I encounter dynamic Christian ministers and ministries that have little or no online communication. We need to hold the Christian community accountable for both the quantity and quality of their online presence. We must develop and use these available tools for the effective propagation of the gospel. We must get good at it. We are the people with the seed of the Word and the world will open up to us like a vulnerable flower waiting to be pollinated.

Where is Martin Luther?

What I find most engaging about this new phenomenon is the ease with which a fifteen-year-old teenage girl can become a published author.

What does this mean for our kids? They are growing up in a world where the Old Boys Club, made up of those who control the media, has been dethroned. Back in the 1980's I attempted to publish my first book, "The Mystery of the Three Days and Nights,"[89] a study of the spiritual side of the death, burial and resurrection of our Lord Jesus Christ. I received only discouragement from the established Christian book publishers. I was told the subject was too controversial and I didn't have a famous name that would sell books. They were right of course, but thanks to the

---

[89] It can be downloaded at www.ChristianThinker.org/books/3days.htm

internet I published my book in 1997 on the web and continue to receive comments from around the world - some good and some scathing. Like Winston Churchill was rumored as saying, "You can write good things about me or bad things, just don't misspell my name."[90] Yes, I was, and to many, still am, very controversial. Nevertheless, I was published and have had significant influence in places I never imagined.

As in the first century the Codex changed the nature of communication, and in the fifteenth century the printing press changed the way communication was distributed, so now, in the twenty-first century we have an unprecedented opportunity. We no longer have to live under the control of those who rule the media.

We are now part of a world, a digital world, which has changed and challenged all of the old world media moguls. Who are the power brokers of knowledge? We could ask Wikipedia,[91] the new free online encyclopedia, whose contributors are anyone who can write about anything. That's right; the largest encyclopedia in the world is made up of articles on anything, from anywhere written by anyone. Don't you need a Ph.D. to write for an encyclopedia? Apparently not. Some of the most prolific writers in this amazing collection of information have no formal education. The material is scrutinized and edited by other non-official officials; anyone, anywhere can edit. Yet what has come forth is an amazing journal and dynamic collection of articles (1,035,558 at the time of this writing).

---

[90] This is one of those quotes that may or may not have been said by a man of so many words. The idea is: for a politician, the most important thing is to get your name out there. It certainly sounds like Churchill.

[91] www.wikipedia.org As you have probably already noted, I quote extensively from this encyclopedia. Formerly, I was a great advocate of the Encyclopedia Britannica because of its trusted scholarship. In recent years, I have found it to be overly authoritative in its approach and difficult to find the answers I need. Wikipedia has been one of the greatest surprises in my scholarly research and attitude. I have found it, time and again, more up to date and informative than Britannica. "Here, here!" to the people's encyclopedia!

Hugh Hewitt is correct in his assessment of the changes around us:

"New technologies in the communication of information bring about radical changes in the existing hierarchies of power and it is never pleasant for those at the top as the Vatican discovered when Luther got his dander up."[92]

The questions I want to leave us with are those I put to the gradating class of 2005 in a sermon I preached on June 25th:

- "Is there is another Martin Luther listening right now?
- "Who will bring the next reformation?
- "Who will stand as a prophet to their generation and the generations to come?
- "Who will combine the genius of the digital world and the next move of God?"

This last question should resonate within us all. The communication revolution means there are still very tough questions that beg for answers:

- Will Christians be able to live free from the pitfalls of this dangerous place called Cyberspace?
- At what level do you block content on your computers?
- Are you learning to email, build websites, blog, and broadcast through RSS and podcast technology?
- What are your family, school and church doing to grow in their ability to communicate digitally?
- Will it be a Christian who finds the next digital innovation?

We are in the biggest communication revolution in all of human history! Like in the first and the fifteenth cen-

---

[92] Hugh Hewitt. *Blog*. Oasis Audio, 2004. Chapter 3, Time 01:53:56

turies we await a Martin Luther. We await a clarion call from the prophet to lead us to the next step that Jesus has for His people. If you have something to say, please step up and answer the call. Perhaps the most important question to this generation is:

"What would Jesus Blog?"

Globalization

"The world is so empty if one thinks only of mountains, rivers and cities; but to know someone here and there who thinks and feels with us, and though distant, is close to us in spirit - this makes the earth for us an inhabited garden"
Johann Wolfgang von Goethe[93]

"Settling in the plush and beautiful plains of Shinar[94] seems to be our destiny" argued Joktan. "Why follow the ramblings of an old man? Why endure the hardship of traveling enormous distances only to work the rest of our days trying to subdue some harsh environment, or worse, see our children starve to death because the barren earth won't give us fruit?"

"God decreed to our great father and his sons that we are to fill the earth," debated his brother Peleg.[95]

---

[93] Johann Wolfgang von Goethe (28 August 1749 – 22 March 1832) was a German polymath: he was a novelist, dramatist, poet, humanist, scientist, philosopher and for ten years, Chief Minister of State at Weimar. http://www.quoteland.com/author.asp?AUTHOR_ID=960
[94] The fictionalized account of this important story in human history is based on Genesis 11:1-9.
[95] Peleg and Joktan became two of the central figures in the Genesis account because of Genesis 10:25 (NIV) *"Two sons were born to Eber: One was named Peleg, because in his time the earth was divided; his brother was named Joktan."*

"Perhaps our great father is too stubborn because of his old age," immediately replied Joktan.

Peleg's response was just as quick "Or perhaps he still fears the God who chose him to survive *the great washing away.*"

"And didn't God also spare our great grandfather, Shem? He didn't argue with the plan, he thinks we should be part of the grand coming together?" responded Joktan.

In fact Shem[96] did not oppose the "coming together." He would listen to his father's objections but wasn't convinced that his was the voice to follow. They had forged out into the new earth almost one hundred years[97] ago just after the great flood but had found nothing but bleak devastation. Hardship awaited them in every region where they had wandered. Shem was right to allow his son, Japheth to take the lead of the clan and bring them to Shinar. He would not let the debate go any further. It was Japheth's decision and Peleg would have to follow his leadership.

The clan of Japheth was the last clan in the entire world to make this trek eastward. When the caravan came to the top of the last hill, the multitude of men, wives and children stopped and gazed in amazement. Only Shem had seen a city made of brick before but nothing that even closely resembled what they were beholding.

The buildings stretched dozens of square miles before them. On the south side of the city rose a great plume of smoke where many brick smelters cooked the blocks into stones. All of the known ways to build did not include what they saw. The slime and pitch from the swamps to the south mixed with mortar from the mountains to the north created a rock-hard substance that rose before them as the new city.[98]

---

[96] Because of the long life spans of men in those days Shem would be about 200 years old. See Genesis 11:10: Shem was 98 at the time of the flood.

[97] One very interesting revelation is how close these events were to the time of the flood. If you follow the chronology of Shem in Genesis 11:10-17, you will find that Peleg was born 101 years after the flood.

[98] I suggest in my story that this is a unique technology. Because scripture emphasizes how they built indicates that it is a significant part of the story.

Japheth's clan was the last to do what all the clans of the earth had being doing for the last decade, committing their effort and family to the vision of the new leader of the earth. They had come to Babel.[99]

The evening after they arrived, a great feast was called in their honor at the center of the city. Babel was built in a ring around a small but gradual rise. This center region was left void of buildings and at the top of the hill that evening, all the peoples of the world finally met together as one great family. It had been over one hundred years of nomadic wandering since they had been together. And now, with all three of the sons of Noah present, the vision had come to pass.

The tall, muscular Nimrod[100] was the last to stride up the gradual slope with his entourage of armed men. His reputation had traveled far and wide for decades among the earth. Whenever news came to the nomads from their distant cousins, it always included tales of the mighty Nimrod. Many late nights were spent around the fires telling the adventures of "the greatest of all hunters before the eyes of God." The messengers would tell how before Nimrod had reached manhood, he saved the clan of Cush from starvation. Cush's clan had wandered too far into the eastern mountains and was trapped by the winter snows only to run out of food. Nimrod had single-handedly hunted and killed a wild and monstrous, hairy beast, bringing it down

---

Genesis 11:3 (NIV) ..."*Come, let's make bricks and bake them thoroughly.*" *They used brick instead of stone, and tar for mortar.*

[99] A picture of the now famous painting can be found online at: Pieter Bruegel the Elder. *The Tower of Babel.* 1563. Oil on panel. Kunsthistorisches Museum, Vienna, Austria. http://www.abcgallery.com/B/bruegel/bruegel50.html It includes the city of Babel surrounding the tower with the exception of water on one side.

[100] Nimrod is central to the building of Babel. Genesis 10:8-10 (NIV) *Cush was the father of Nimrod, who grew to be a mighty warrior on the earth. He was a mighty hunter before the LORD; that is why it is said, "Like Nimrod, a mighty hunter before the LORD." The first centers of his kingdom were Babylon, Erech, Akkad and Calneh, in Shinar.* (Babylon was originally called Babel.)

with both his bow and spear. It had provided food for the entire winter to the tables of the starving families.

His reputation distinguished him as more than just the greatest hunter of the earth. In the years to follow, all the clans had selected and sent at least one of their strongest young men to train under Nimrod. They would return to their families with more than new skills to hunt. They would return as disciples of this charismatic leader. They would bring Nimrod's new vision for humanity. His plan was to end the wanderings of the scattered people to work together as one family and build a people, a culture and a city that even God would not be able to stop.

Even Peleg seemed to be swept away with Nimrod's compelling vision delivered in his speech that night. The great leader called for all the peoples of the earth to lay aside their claims to various regions. He called for all differences to be settled. His words were full of passion, desire and direction. They were sure words, full of command and vision, something which all the clans seemed to lack. Peleg remembered feeling this way once before when he had heard the great patriarch, Noah speak to his clan, though the message had been very different. Noah had commanded them to go into all the earth, to rebuild and replenish the wastelands.[101] Noah had spoken with as much passion that a man of his ancient years could muster. If only he were here now, perhaps Peleg would not be as swept away with this new vision for mankind.

Nimrod's preaching to this global gathering was full of fire and great oratory. Truly he had become so much more than a "great hunter." He had become mankind's great leader. His speech ended with a stunning call to action.

"The great sons of Noah, our fathers," he exclaimed, "have brought us all together to this great vision. Years ago in our wanderings we came upon the clan of Sidon, son of Canaan. They had discovered one of the old world arts of

---

[101] This comes from the commission that God gave Noah and his sons when they left the ark. Genesis 9:1 (NIV) *Then God blessed Noah and his sons, saying to them, "Be fruitful and increase in number and fill the earth."*

making brick and begun to build homes. Using this new method had caused others to fear the wrath of God and so they had been banished from the other clans. They had separated from their cousins out of fear for their lives. Nevertheless, this new technology created a safe place from the elements. Their way of life changed and their families prospered. We have improved upon their technology by adding special ingredients from this region." Nimrod's voice began to rise. "Now we can build a great city in this place of prosperity. We can create a place for all of mankind to dwell together under one vision and one voice." His face flushed red with passion. "What of the God of Noah? What of His call to scatter? What of the danger of judgment? We will make a place for ourselves in His Temple in Heaven. We will build a tower that will reach into His Heaven; a tower so strong, made with our new technology, which He cannot tear down with wind or storm; a tower so tall that He cannot cover it with the waters as in the time of old.[102] And then He will love us and He will give us a name – we will be the children of God – we will be his people again."[103] Everyone was standing now, even the elders, waiting for the next words of Nimrod, all waiting for this new vision that would transform their existence. "We will build it here on this very spot!"

The multitude exploded in exultant cheers. In unison the whole earth chanted, "He will give us a name! He will give us a name! He will give us a name..."

As those around him were caught up in the frenzy, Peleg knew what he had to do. The next day he gathered

---

[102] I offer this idea as a possible motive for building such a high tower. Because the flood was still very much a part of their consciousness, it is possible that they would seek to avoid this judgment again.

[103] Genesis 11:4 (NIV) *Then they said, "Come, let us build ourselves a city, with a tower that reaches to the heavens, so that we may make a name for ourselves and not be scattered over the face of the whole earth."* This indicates that their motive was beyond escaping judgment. Their desire to make a name for themselves is interesting seeing that they were all gathering in one place. I suggest that this need for fame is their desire to reach out to God. Their desire to gather together and escape judgment is connected to this new name they sought.

his wife and small children and left the plush plains of Shinar. He refused to blaspheme the God of Noah. He would not be a part of this abomination. No one else joined him.

Decades of collaboration, communication and work transforming this new technology yielded the most astonishing structure. The city and tower continued to be the unifying force for humanity. Joktan's sons had been small children when they first arrived; now they were the new generation of foremen shaping new methods and techniques that enabled them to build a stronger city and a higher tower. They grew up as city dwellers and city builders. Thanks to the mighty Nimrod, their families had a much safer, easier life. This new generation of youth developed many new technologies for efficient communication, transportation and growth as the city and the people of the earth stretched out. At the center of it was the great tower. It spiraled high into the skies of Shinar, competing with the distant mountains for the skyline view. Surely God and his messengers would take note.

God and his messengers did take note![104] It began with a long-forgotten voice. In a cart driven by Peleg, who had not been in Babel for over two decades, a very old man was brought into the city. Rue, Peleg's son steadied the old man as the cart jostled through the streets. As they entered the city, this ancient preacher began to stir as in the days before the flood. The great father, Noah,[105] had come to Babel to speak the Word of God to his children.

They drove directly to the large, central home of Nimrod. Out of respect for his great-grandfather, Nimrod allowed Noah to speak to his descendents in spite of the contrary vision he would bring. Since construction had begun on the tower, the massive square in front of Nimrod's home served as the people's gathering place. It was large enough to host the thousands of men who would assemble

---

[104] Genesis 11:5 (NIV) *But the LORD came down to see the city and the tower that the men were building.*

[105] The scripture does not indicate any involvement of Noah in the dividing of the peoples. However, the time-lines indicate clearly that Noah was still alive at this time. Genesis 9:28 (NIV) *After the flood Noah lived 350 years.*

and then return to their families with the latest direction. That afternoon the bells rang, calling for the assembly of men to meet with the oldest living patriarch.

Though Noah was ancient and frail he projected his voice to the crowd in deep, foreboding tones. Noah belted out with all his strength, "My wayward children, what have you done? You have disobeyed the God of all creation. You have built for yourselves a name, but that name is evil! You have come together as one. Everything you speak is with one voice. Now nothing is impossible for your evil heart to create. Thus God will come down from heaven and He will bring distraction and confusion among you."[106]

While Noah was speaking, Joktan pushed his way to the front of the crowd and motioned to speak. Peleg, recognizing his brother, placed his hand on Noah and brought the prophet's attention to his great-great-grandson. Noah motioned to Joktan to come and speak. Before he began, Noah shouted to crowd with the assurance that could only come with divine foresight, "It will end right here."

Joktan turned to address the crowd, "People of Babel, the mighty Nimrod has given us unity! Our children have grown in safety. Our clans are one!" As Joktan spoke, a stir broke out in the crowd. He continued, "Look what we have been able to do. Look at what our children have become." They looked at each other and then at Joktan confused and bewildered. One of Joktan's sons pushed his way to the cart and told him that those of the other clans were babbling and speaking nonsense. Joktan turned to Peleg but even his own brother looked at him with surprise. Peleg could understand some of what Joktan had said but with the strange sounds mixed in, Peleg couldn't make sense of it.

The crowd dispersed in confusion almost as fast as it had come together. Throughout the streets of Babel, fights broke out as people could not understand each other's in-

---

[106] Genesis 11:6-7 (NIV) *The LORD said, "If as one people speaking the same language they have begun to do this, then nothing they plan to do will be impossible for them. Come, let us go down and confuse their language so they will not understand each other."*

tentions. Confusion reigned in Babel and all progress came to a halt.

Days passed and Nimrod called another assembly but even the "the greatest of all hunters before the eyes of God" could not communicate with any more than a small number of his people. He turned to Father Noah and asked him to speak to his people. Nimrod called Babel's last great assembly. When the crowd was assembled, Noah, by God's intervention, was able to speak to them all. This was the last time that all of mankind together understood words spoken in one language. "Go out into all the world, by God's grace, rebuild the wastelands, be fruitful, multiply and re-plenish the earth."

The First Worldwide Movement

My fictionalized account of this amazing story of Babel reveals man's heart toward globalization. Here is the Biblical version from the New International Version:

[1] Now the whole world had one language and a common speech. [2] As men moved eastward, they found a plain in Shinar and settled there. [3] They said to each other, "Come, let's make bricks and bake them thoroughly." They used brick instead of stone, and tar for mortar. [4] Then they said, "Come, let us build ourselves a city, with a tower that reaches to the heavens, so that we may make a name for ourselves and not be scattered over the face of the whole earth." [5] But the LORD came down to see the city and the tower that the men were building. [6] The LORD said, "If as one people speaking the same language they have begun to do this, then nothing they plan to do will be impossible for them. [7] Come, let us go down and confuse their language so they will not understand each other." [8] So the LORD scattered them from there over all the earth, and they stopped building the city. [9] That is why it was called Babel —because there the LORD confused

the language of the whole world. From there the LORD
scattered them over the face of the whole earth.

Genesis 11:1-9.

We can learn several important ideas about global-ization from this story.

First, common communication is absolutely neces-sary for true globalization to occur. In the world of Babel, everyone spoke the same language; this, obviously, facili-tated cooperation on a level that has not been achieved since.

We are closer today than the thousands of years since Babel to a one-world language. This can be seen by the worldwide dominance of the English language.[107] Eng-lish is easily the most widely spoken language in the world. It ranks third for native speakers at 380 million behind Chinese and Hindi. But it is in first position as the most widely spoken, second language in the world. Through the global influence of cinema, airlines, broadcasting, science and the internet, English is now required in many fields and occupations around the world. English scholar and poet, Walt Whitman, speaks about the ability of English to accommodate a world wide usage:

"Viewed freely, the English language is the accretion and growth of every dialect, race, and range of time, and is both the free and compacted composition of all."[108]

One could make a case for the new digital language becoming a possible one-world means of communication. It has given us the means to speak to one another even if not in the same language. It is only a matter of time until translation programs will work as seamlessly as in *Star Trek*. In our campus school, we have had the privilege of

---

[107] Some interesting statistics can be found at:
http://en.wikipedia.org/wiki/English_language
[108] Ed Folsom. *Walt Whitman's Native Representations*. Cambridge Univer-sity Press, May 1997. Page 17.

receiving international students who have succeeded in bridging this language gap with the aid of pocket translators that are no bigger than the average calculator.

The second lesson we learn from the first movement toward globalization is the crucial role technology plays in bringing people together. "Come, let's make bricks and bake them thoroughly." This may not seem like earth shattering technology, no pun intended, but when you consider that all of mankind had been nomadic since the flood, the idea of solid, brick buildings is revolutionary. A new technology gave birth to a new way of coming together. In today's global world, technology, again, is a unifying factor in bringing us together.

Finally, we see a shift in worldview made evident by the contrary direction the world went from the commandment given to Noah and his sons. At some point in the one hundred years of history between the flood and Babel, people's view of the world shifted dramatically. They gave up on God's command to *"fill the earth."* As I have shown in my fictional rendition of these events, they were not just getting tired of a nomadic lifestyle. There was a shift in the spiritual aspect of their worldview that brought them together. As illustrated, Nimrod connected the human race to his new vision of humanity. God had given a powerful command to Noah after the cataclysmic example of His judgment on the earth. In a short period of time, the entire human race went in the opposite direction. Only a global alteration in worldview could bring about such global change.

Today we find ourselves experiencing similar examples of globalization. We see our world moving toward one language, inspired by global shifts in our worldview, carried on the back of the internet. Could this be our tower?

According to the KOF Index of Globalization,[109] based on economic, social and political data, the United

---

[109] "The index measures the three main dimensions of globalization: economic, social, and political. In addition to three indices measuring these dimensions, we calculate an overall index of globalization and sub-indices referring to actual economic flows, economic restrictions, data on personal

States and Canada are the two most "globalized" countries in the world. This means that we are the most connected multicultural, pluralistic, free and democratic cultures on the planet. It could also mean that we are the Babel of today. Are we, like the people of Nimrod, trying to *"make a name for ourselves and not be scattered over the face of the whole earth."*[110] One thing is for sure – the world is changing and it started here.

Globalization 1.0, 2.0 and 3.0

In Thomas Friedman's landmark book, *The World is Flat - A Brief History of the Twenty-First Century*, he describes three periods of Globalization. The years 1492-1800 he marks as the first period, or "Globalization 1.0." Obviously, this period started when Christopher Columbus discovered the new world. This was the period of global expansion and imperialism. It was when the nation-states, as we know them today, were born. This period was driven by national expansion. Friedman writes:

"...in Globalization 1.0 the key agent of change, the dynamic force driving the process of global integration was how much brawn - how much muscle, how much horsepower, wind power, or, later, steam power – your country had and how creatively you could deploy it. In this era, countries and governments (often inspired by religion or imperialism or a combination of both) led the way in breaking down walls and knitting the world together, driving global integration."[111]

---

contact, data on information flows, and data on cultural proximity. Data are available on a yearly basis for 123 countries over the period 1970-2003." Dreher, Axel. *Does Globalization Affect Growth? Evidence from a new Index of Globalization.* KOF Konjunkturforschungsstelle, 2006 http://www.globalization-index.org/

[110] Genesis 11:4 (NIV)

[111] Thomas L. Friedman. *The World Is Flat: A Brief History of the Twenty-first Century.* Farrar, Straus and Giroux, 2005. Page 9. This is a best-selling book by Thomas L. Friedman analyzing the progress of globalization in the early twenty-first century.

The church was reluctant to embrace the idea of global expansion. The Roman Catholic Church had gone on record that it still believed in a flat world. It had rejected the scientific ideas of Copernicus and Galileo. Yet, it wasn't long after Columbus returned with news of the new world that the views of the church changed. The church grudgingly adopted the idea of a round world and became very influential in how the new, expanding world was shaped. Later, Protestants saw the new world as an opportunity to escape the autocratic rule of the Roman Church in Europe and comprised most of the early pilgrims to North America.

Friedman's idea of "Globalization 2.0" is the period from 1800 till 2000. He describes this era as the time when multinational companies came of age. He writes:

"In Globalization 2.0, the key agent of change, the dynamic force driving global integration, was multinational companies. These multinationals went global for markets and labor...In the first half of the this era, global integration was powered by falling transportation costs, thanks to the steam engine and the railroad, and in the second half by falling telecommunication costs... It was during this era that we really saw the birth and maturation of a global economy, in the sense that there was enough movement of goods and information from continent to continent for there to be a global market, with global arbitrage in products and labor."[112]

Friedman characterizes the world as going from large to medium in "Globalization 1.0" then from medium to small in version "2.0." Finally in "Globalization 3.0," beginning around the year 2000, he says the transformation went from "a size small to a size tiny." He continues:

---

[112] Ibid., page 9-10.

"...the dynamic force in Globalization 3.0 – the thing that gives it its unique character – is the newfound power for *individuals* to collaborate and compete globally. And the lever that is enabling individuals and groups to go global so easily and so seamlessly is not horsepower, and not hardware, but software – all sorts of new applications – in conjunction with the creation of a global fiber-optic network that has made us all next-door neighbors."[113]

Friedman goes on to describe "ten forces that flattened the world" or, to paraphrase, ten reasons that made the world an even playing field for everyone. These ten reasons are a combination of political changes in our world such as the fall of communism and the opening up of world markets, the economic rise of India, China and other developing nations and the convergence of key communication technologies. Over and over he makes a very strong argument that the world is, indeed, becoming very flat.

No More Borders

The global world is here due to the advent of these amazing technologies. It means that there are no more borders. You can, with the ease of using your mouse and keyboard, relate to people all over the earth.

If you have ever played online games, you know that you can compete on a world stage. For almost a year, several of our young people played an online game called "GunBound." This somewhat harmless game of precision canon shooting has worldwide participation. Simply sign up, download the program and start shooting. There is an online ranking system where most of the top "GunBound" players are in eastern Asia. I viewed a game being played by Dan Knorr, our school chaplain, with players on three continents. Simultaneously, Dan was able to communicate

---

[113] Ibid., page 10.

and play a game in real-time with gamers in Japan, Brazil and the U.S. What is so remarkable about this is not the simple game he was playing; it was that, until five years ago, this level of communication and mutual participation on such a global scale had never been available, not in all of human history.

It is likely in the last couple of years that you have spoken with someone from India, or more precisely, Bangalore, India, the outsourcing capital of the world. If you have placed an order for a major brand-name computer over the phone or have been in need of technical support, then you have probably been routed to a salesperson or technician in India. Perhaps you have been interrupted by a telephone solicitor; many of those calls are now coming from India. This is known as "outsourcing." It is when a cheaper, often more efficient, workforce is used remotely to meet the needs of a company. In "Globalization 2.0," supply chains for goods and commodities were frequently outsourced. But today, even basic services are part of the global supply chain.

Terrorists have figured this out. Al Qaeda has developed a worldwide communication network allowing its members and cells to move without detection in any country of the world. This has changed the very concept of warfare in our world. A handful of operatives can wreck havoc on the world's superpower. The internet has become a vital tool in terrorist activities and recruitment. Freelance journalist and author, Lawrence Wright, wrote in an article published in *The New Yorker* magazine:

"The Internet provides confused young Muslims in Europe with a virtual community. Those who cannot adapt to their new homes discover on the Internet a responsive and compassionate forum... Gabriel Weimann, a senior fellow at the United States Institute of Peace, has been monitoring terrorist Web sites for seven years. 'When we started, there were only twelve sites,' he told me. 'Now there are more than four thousand.' Every known terrorist group maintains more than one Web site, and often the sites are in different languages. "You can download music, videos, donate money, receive training,' Weimann said. 'It's a virtual training camp.'"[114]

Thankfully, the Christian church is also figuring this out. The internet has become the fastest growing medium for North Americans seeking faith related answers. In a study by the Barna Group, an evangelical think tank, published on March 14th, 2005, they monitored religious uses of the media. This is what they found regarding internet usage:

"A decade ago, faith-related websites were not on the radar screen of Americans. That is changing in a hurry, however. Today, one out of every six adults (16%) spends some time visiting faith-oriented websites during a typical month. This is especially common among evangelicals: 41% visit such sites, compared to 18% of all other born again Christians and 10% of non-born again Americans."[115]

Recently I downloaded an interesting radio documentary called "Global 3.0." Journalist, Robert Krulwich, and American RadioWorks economics editor, Chris Farrell, examined how the high-speed movement of goods, people, capital, and ideas is transforming the global economy and life in our own backyard. They told the story of how globalization is changing lives from Pittsburg to Bangladesh. They closed the program with these comments that succinctly describe the possibilities of globalized communication:

---

[114] Laurence Wright. *The Terror Web*. Originally published in *The New Yorker* magazine 2 August 2004. It can be found at Laurence Wright's website at: http://www.lawrencewright.com/art-madrid.html
[115] The Barna Group. *More People Use Christian Media Than Attend Church*. The Barna Update. 14 March 2005
http://www.barna.org/FlexPage.aspx?Page=BarnaUpdate&BarnaUpdateID=184

"There is now the opportunity for people who want to know, who are curious to find out about pretty much everything and that's a big difference. If we are look-ing for the one really fundamental change about glob-alization, it is that there are now highways for people to whisper to each other, to pursue ideas, to seek in-formation. And while there are dictatorships that will try to cut you off at the pass and there are things about human beings that are mean and will never go away, here is something new: a chance to whisper to the whole world. That to me is a very big change."[116]

Who is My Neighbor?

Jesus was asked this question in a conversation with a lawyer about what he must do to receive eternal life. The answer that any learned Jew would make was "...*Love the Lord your God with all your heart and with all your soul and with all your strength and with all your mind;" and, "Love your neighbor as yourself."*[117] Trying to trap Jesus in a slip of theology, the lawyer took it a step further and asked, "Who is my neighbor?" Jesus then gives us the fa-mous story about a robbery and beating and who would help this beaten man. The religious elite did not help him. The busy bureaucrat did not help him. It was the Samari-tan, a Jewish half-breed, who was the true neighbor. He went way out of his way to help this hurting man.

Jesus defined a loving neighbor as one who helps those in need. In our world of fast, convenient transporta-tion and worldwide communication, our neighbor is proba-bly not the person who lives next door.

---

[116]Robert Krulwich and Chris Farrell. *Global 3.0.* American Radio Works 1 March 2006. Podcast through RSS feeds. I downloaded it from Audi-ble.com.
[117]Luke 10:27 (NIV). Luke 10:25-37 is known as the parable of the Good Samaritan. Jesus teaches what it truly means to "love your neighbor as yourself."

In the new global world your neighbor may live in China, as my brother discovered.

In spiritual matters, my little brother, Ken, has always been more of a big brother to me. He was very instrumental in leading me to Christ. He was my first true discipler, getting me started in a serious devotion to learning the Word in my early years as a believer. He has always been committed to following the Lord, often in some very interesting directions. Thanks to our dad, Ken and I both developed an interest in computers. Ken has always stayed up-to-date with the latest computer technology for the purpose of studying the Word. He always had the latest and greatest computer with the most sophisticated Bible Software he could find. In the nineties, Ken found Logos Bible Software[118] and began to work on ways he could use their materials more efficiently. In the year 2000, a dream began to form in his mind. *We could use this to reach people who are without the Word of God. We could reach China!*

In 2001, Ken started the Digital Bible Society[119] and is its president to this day. Their vision posted on their website sounds like the first chapter of this book.

"In the twentieth century another printing press came on the scene – the personal computer. And in the space of two decades, the PC dramatically transformed the economic and social order of our world. But the revolution is just beginning. … We believe another reformation is at hand. Huge segments of the world community are still without Bibles and Christian literature. In China alone, the Bible League estimates that some 45 million Christians still do not have a Bible they can call their own. We believe the new 'printing press,' will change everything. …

---

[118] http://www.logos.com/ This is probably the most scholarly Bible software on the market today. It is also one of the most expensive.
[119] http://www.digitalbiblesociety.org/ You can learn much more about this project here. You can join the Society, donate finances and order CD's for distribution at this website.

"We purpose to assist in the worldwide distribution of digital Christian media that every believer in every nation will have free access to explore and understand the Scriptures in their own language - whether through the printed page, the spoken word (audio), or visual presentation (video)."[120]

These were ambitious goals for an air traffic controller living in Spring, Texas. Ken was not a part of a worldwide mission's network. He was not the head of some dynamic TV ministry. Ken is a guy who loves the Word of God and knew enough about digital communication to get this started. To date, they have distributed over 30,000 CDs in China and Taiwan. But it hasn't stopped there. I estimate that for every CD produced over 100 copies are distributed. When a CD makes its way to a pastor, he is encouraged to make copies for everyone in his congregation and then encourages them to distribute the Word to anyone who will take it. The Chinese are the world's greatest copyright violators; so making copies comes naturally to them. The great thing about digital technology is that it suffers almost no degradation in the copying process. One CD can be copied to another then the copy can be copied and so on. A copy made from ten generations of other copies will yield the same quality of data as the original.

This technology has facilitated a global distribution of the Word of God in the Chinese language. Recently, one of the Society's partners was visiting a Chinese-speaking church in Panama. He discovered that they had distributed the Bible CD to all of their members. Another partner visited a similar church in Brazil. He went to install the software on the pastor's computer only to find a more current version of the software already installed.

They are just getting ready to release Version 4.0 in both Chinese and Arabic! It will have hundreds of disciple-

---

[120] *Digital Bible Society Vision*. Digital Bible Society. 5 April 2006. http://www.digitalbiblesociety.org/vision.htm and *Digital Bible Society Mission*. Digital Bible Society. 5 April 2006. http://www.digitalbiblesociety.org/mission.htm

ship training books, *The Hope Video* built into the software that integrates with the scriptures, 476 worship songs, three versions of the Chinese Bible and a multitude of commentaries and dictionaries.

When finishing my interview with Ken about the Digital Bible project he quoted me from a conversation we had years ago:

> "You said to me years ago, Greg, 'Every generation has a sound. In order to reach that generation you must learn the sound and fill it with the Word of God.' The world becomes smaller every day – it really is a new digital generation – they learn differently and think differently. *The new Global sound is Digital.*"

In a global world, with instant communication and transportation that puts any part of the world within a day's reach, we have a huge responsibility to love our neighbor. It is a great transgression of Jesus' command when Christians stay ignorant of the world around them.

Recently, our church became aware of horrible crimes against the children of Uganda from the personality-driven cult called the Lord's Resistance Army (LRA).[121] Within weeks of learning about this terrible plight, our mission's chairman booked a flight to Uganda. He visited a dynamic Christian mission that works with multiple NGOs[122] to help solve this terrible problem. Jerry and Can-

---

[121] *Lord's Resistance Army.* Wikipedia, The Free Encyclopedia. 5 April 2006 19:55 UTC http://en.wikipedia.org/wiki/Lord's_Resistance_Army "The Lord's Resistance Army (LRA), formed in 1987, is a rebel paramilitary group operating mainly in northern Uganda. The group is engaged in an armed rebellion against the Ugandan government in what is now one of Africa's longest-running conflicts. It is led by Joseph Kony, who proclaims himself a spirit medium, and apparently wishes to establish a state based on his unique interpretation of Biblical millenarianism. The LRA have been accused of widespread human rights violations, including the abduction of civilians, the use of child soldiers and a number of massacres."

[122] NGO – Non Government Organizations are typically non-profit organizations working in the third world to bring aid.

dis Bingham[123] are called to this war-torn region of Uganda. They work with fellow Ugandan Christians to deliver the Gospel and serve the huge needs that this civil war has caused. Our church hopes to build an entire village for young mothers and orphaned children. I hope to use part of the proceeds from this book for this cause. Our "neighbor" is now a little Ugandan boy who has been kidnapped by the LRA and forced to do unspeakable things.

This is just one of thousands of places around the globe that is aching for the Church to respond. In this digital world, we now have global responsibilities unlike any other time in human history.

Global Government or Not

As the world becomes more and more digital, it is only a matter of time until it begins to destabilize government structures around the world. We have seen how terrorists can travel freely in cyberspace but there are similar examples of how those under totalitarian governments can slip from their grasp through cyberspace.

During the civil war in Kosovo, story after story emerged of how people escaped the Serbian occupation and mass executions.[124] Several organizations dedicated to free speech on the net helped the beleaguered people of Kosovo get word out to the rest of the world by setting up an internet server, named anonomizer.com, which facilitated blogs from Kosovo. However, the best communication out of Kosovo was straightforward email. The best known story is about the email correspondence between Adona, an ethnic Albanian sixteen year old girl, and Finnegan Hammel, a

---

[123] The Bingham's work through Action International can be viewed at http://www.actionintl.org/action

[124] In the digital audio book, *The Hacker Ethic and the Spirit of the New Economy* Pekka Himanen tells story after story of how digital technology is changing the way people around the world are using the internet to escape the confines of government control. You can download the book at www.audible.com.

student at Berkley High School in California. She wrote many emails telling of the atrocities taking place all around her.

Her graphic story told through this medium was immediately posted on blogs and sent around the internet via email. It is thought that her explicit emails focused the attention of thousands of Americans and Europeans on the calamity in Kosovo and then they forced their governments to act. This led to the NATO air strikes in Kosovo and Serbia. What made this communication so crucial at the time was the crackdown on journalists all over Yugoslavia that made reporting the atrocities very difficult. In the globalized world, the Serbian officials couldn't find nor stop the digital communication of a sixteen year old girl.

Globalized freedom of communication will eventually cause enormous, tsunami-like shifts to occur throughout the governments of the world. A tsunami, when it begins out in the ocean, is a four or five foot wave. It covers a vast area and is a huge displacement of water; it can be easily navigated by ships at sea. But when it comes close to the shore, the mass of water moving inland has devastating effects. The undersea quake of the communication revolution has already happened. The tsunami is moving steadily toward the shorelines of the world's governments and everything is about to change. It may take only one girl sending consistent email reports to topple a government.

As I was writing this chapter I received an email for a study being done at the University of British Columbia. The email called for the participation of teachers who would consider themselves part of the "anti-globalization movement."

There are many forces around the world trying to stop the move toward globalization. Surely, any totalitarian government would fear losing control of their people's ability to share ideas freely. China is going through these types of difficult issues. Consider that it is the fastest growing economy in the world yet their government still uses many of the structures put in place by Chairman Mao. The need for China to globalize its communication systems is countered by the need to control what their people are allowed to know and communicate. They have worked very hard to establish an extensive internet filtering system called, by critics in the west, "the great firewall of China." My brother's website for the Digital Bible Society has been blocked because they posted information about persecuted Chinese believers.

Public debate is not uncommon in countries like Canada and the U.S. National pride is often objectionable to globalization. Keeping jobs for our own people instead of outsourcing is a strong argument. With the new threat of terrorism to our way of life, stronger surveillance measures are being used that pose a threat to our privacy.

As Christians how are we to respond to global changes?

Let's Not Forget our Christian Mandate

I am often very surprised by the way many evangelicals have responded to globalization. Evangelicals from my Christian persuasion tend to go in two directions.

The most frequent response comes from the reigning eschatological perspective best told in Jerry Jenkins and Tim LeHaye's "Left Behind" book series. This theology of the end times came into vogue about 170 years ago in the height of the Dispensationalism[125] movement in the church. Dispensationalism is the theological perspective that di-

---

[125] An exceptional article on the topic with views presented for and against Dispensationalism can be found at: *Dispensationalism*. Wikipedia, The Free Encyclopedia. 29 March 2006 20:37 UTC http://en.wikipedia.org/wiki/Dispensationalism "Dispensationalism is a conceptual overview and interpretive framework for understanding the overall flow of the Bible. As a branch of Christian theology, it teaches biblical history as a number of successive economies or administrations under God known as "dispensations," and emphasizes the continuity of the Old Testament covenants God made with the Jewish people through Abraham, Moses and King David. Dispensationalist Christian eschatology emphasizes a premillennial futurist view of prophecy of the "end times" and a pretribulation view of the rapture."

vides up history into periods. The period following the current age is called the tribulation, a seven-year period of judgment when the antichrist is revealed and takes control of a one-world government. Therefore, globalization is one of the necessary steps for the end of this age to come. It is taught that this will be followed by the physical return of Christ to rule over the earth for 1000 years. Usually the debate in our circles is about *when* Jesus will come for the church. The post-tribulationist teaches that Jesus will return and rapture the church away after the seven years; the pre-tribulationist argues that the rapture will take place before the seven-year tribulation, thus the idea of the non-believers "left behind." There is therefore a subtle resistance in the heart of the Christian adhering to this eschatology, to support globalization, which will ultimately bring in the anti-Christ.

The other recent tendency of evangelicals, in North America particularly, is the strong influence toward nationalism. Because Christians have lost so many ethical and moral debates in the last few years, we have renewed the call to participate politically and culturally. Naturally our pulpits have used patriotic symbols and rhetoric to inspire people to action. It isn't uncommon in our church for someone to wave the nation's flag. This sense of nationalism will often divert our focus from the commission that Jesus gave us to go out into all the world.

On the eve of our federal election, I had the opportunity to address our church on the matter of voting and participation in the political process. I tried to remind our congregation that we are Christians who live in Canada, not Canadians who happen to be Christian. Of course, I declared that we should vote as long as our earthly governments allow us to. But, our vote should not be based upon what is best for Canada, rather what is best for the kingdom of God.

Let me return to the "alien" metaphor from my chapter on Discipleship.[126] We are not of this world; we are an

---

[126] See pages 50-52.

alien race of people called to influence this planet for the purposes of our alien King, Jesus. He has called us to bring the Word of God and the power of His love to a world that is opposed to His Kingdom. The human governments of the world are often opposed to our message and methods because, ultimately, our King will bring those governments down when he returns.

Now, we find ourselves in this world with an opportunity to influence it on a global scale. It is time for the church to formulate a response toward globalization:

- What about the lesson from Babel – perhaps God is still against the idea of globalization?
- What should be our response to the fallen people of our planet coming together *as one people speaking the same language?"*
- Do we still think in small, regional boundaries?
- How does a globalized world change our homes, schools and churches?
- What should the church be outsourcing and what services can we provide on a global scale?
- What strategies do we have as churches to go global?
- To what level should we support globalization – even if it hurts our native countries?
- Are our allegiances to territories, economies and governments or to the kingdom of God?
- How can we use the digital pathways of the world to accomplish the task of worldwide discipleship?

Jesus said to go into all the world. Perhaps for us, the redeemed - the alien race of those in Christ - globalization will be the means we can use to bring the Gospel to the fallen peoples of this planet. Now we can do this from the comfort of our living room.

Informationalism

The next best thing to knowing something is to know where to find it.

Samuel Johnson[127]

In 1979, when Sergey Brin was five years old, his family decided to leave Moscow. They were weary of the anti-Semitism both his mother and father were facing as academic and scientist. Sergey's father is a mathematician and his mother is a rocket scientist. They found a way to come to the land of opportunity.[128]

Unlike most immigrants to America, Sergey's family quickly found excellent career opportunities. His father became a professor of mathematics at the University of Maryland and his mother eventually used her specialty at NASA.

---

[127] "Samuel Johnson, L.L.D. (September 7, 1709 to December 13, 1784), often referred to simply as Dr. Johnson, was one of England's greatest literary figures: poet, essayist, biographer, lexicographer, and often esteemed as the finest literary critic in English. Johnson was a great wit and prose stylist of genius, whose bons mots are still frequently quoted in print today." *Dr Samuel Johnson.* Wikipedia, The Free Encyclopedia. 4 April 2006 19:42 UTC http://en.wikipedia.org/wiki/Samuel_Johnson

[128] Both Sergey Brin's and Larry Page's early biographies are told in *The Google Story* by David A. Vise. Random House Audible, November 2005. This is the official Google story and makes Sergey and Larry out to be the saviors of the internet world. A much better critical book where I did most of my research on the topic was *The Search* by John Battelle. Penguin Group Publishers, 8 September 2005.

When Sergey was nine, he received his first computer, a Commodore 64. It wasn't long before his genius for mathematics and computing was apparent to all. He left high school early and enrolled in his father's university. When his Science Degree was complete, he moved on to Stanford University and by August 1995, received his Master's Degree in computer science, again ahead of schedule. He began his doctoral program without a true sense of direction. He couldn't seem to find a project that satisfied his blended skills and interest, until he met Larry.

Larry Page was born in Lansing, Michigan, also to academic parents. Larry's father is a professor of computer science and his mother teaches programming. Both are part of the faculty at Michigan State University.

Larry grew up as the typical geekie kid at school which made him somewhat of an introvert. He was often compared to Bill Gates as he possessed some of Gates' nerdish quirks. Larry even looks a bit like Bill Gates; not a bad thing when your whole life revolves around computers.

Like Sergey, Larry attended his parent's university where he received his Bachelor of Science degree. He transferred, at the end of his Master's program, to Stanford. When he arrived at the school, he was given the standard tour of the campus and its programs from a second year student. That student was Sergey Brin.

Sergey and Larry did not hit if off in the way that you would expect, having so much in common. In fact, they argued and fought the entire tour and, for the next few days, over almost every topic they discussed. Nevertheless, this guy seemed to challenge Sergey and it wasn't long before he considered teaming up with Larry for their Doctoral project. What they did agreed upon was the significant place the internet was taking in their digital culture. They dreamed about how to make it useful. They began their project which eventually put their academic pursuits on hold.[129] Together they launched one of the most successful technology companies of all time, Google Inc.

---

[129] http://www-db.stanford.edu/~backrub/google.html This was the final paper written by Page and Brin. Even though they never finished their doc-

And Then There Was Google

At the time of their arrival at Stanford, the internet was gaining momentum in the commercial world but still had its roots in the academic world. Academia's biggest complaint was trying to find information on the web. The internet was a great research tool if you could find the papers specific to your field of study. If you entered a search term into one of the most common search tools such as Altavista,[130] multiple links would show up that had no relevance to your topic. Research on the web was still very time-consuming and often led to page after page of useless information.

Larry Page and Sergey Brin worked to solve this problem by developing a method of ranking webpages based upon how they linked to other pages and how other pages linked to them. The challenge was to back-link pages.[131] It was easy to count how many links a page went out to, but to discover everyone who was linking in to a particular page became very difficult. And ranking the significance of the page-linking to the website was a huge mathematical challenge. Page and Brin developed programming called Page-Rank[132] to do this work.

---

torate studies, it continues to be one of the most accessed research papers at Stanford University. It details their approach to searching on the internet and introduces the prototype of Google.

[130] http://www.altavista.com/ This was the favored search tool of the mid-nineties.

[131] Larry Page originally called his initial programming "Backrub" based on going back through the net to see who linked to a particular webpage. Today this type of program is called a webcrawler.

[132] Google. *Google searches more sites more quickly, delivering the most relevant results.* 4 April 2006 http://www.google.com/technology/ "PageRank relies on the uniquely democratic nature of the web by using its vast link structure as an indicator of an individual page's value. In essence, Google interprets a link from page A to page B as a vote, by page A, for page B. But, Google looks at more than the sheer volume of votes, or links a page receives; it also analyzes the page that casts the vote. Votes cast by

The next step of this process was to "crawl" the web in order to collect the data of links necessary to rank the pages. They begged, borrowed and stole as much hardware as they could possibly use for this task at Stanford. They started their web crawler, called Backrub, on Larry's own webpage and it went out into the net. They quickly discovered that this was a much bigger undertaking than they originally thought. Their hard drives rapidly filled with data and there seemed to be no end to it. At one point, half of Stanford's computer resources were being tasked for this work.

Among the University insiders, the new search tool, dubbed "Google,"[133] was a big hit. The ability to index and search the University's knowledge and the growing number of links became a very useful tool, yet not without its challenges.

A major side effect was the difficulties the web crawler created in the outside world. At the time, webmasters and companies didn't have a huge desire to be searched. They were suspicious that their intellectual property was being stolen. Also, entire servers were shutting down because of the load placed on them by Stanford's computers. By the time one quarter of the internet was cataloged, Brin and Page were being gently pushed out of Stanford. It was just too much for the University. Stanford's computer network, one of the most sophisticated in the world, was also straining under the load and on one occasion ground to a halt because of Google's ambitious web-crawling.

Another side effect started to emerge as Google began to be used outside of the confines of Stanford. Outsiders were finding Google helpful but complaints started to come in regarding where sites were ranked on Google. At first this was mostly an academic complaint but businesses were

---

pages that are themselves 'important' weigh more heavily and help to make other pages 'important.'"

[133] Google is a misspelled version of "googol." The dictionary.com definition is: "The number 10 raised to the power 100 (10^{100}), written out as the numeral 1 followed by 100 zeros."

also taking note. Google was beginning to shake up the internet. In *The Search,* by John Battelle, he remarks on this ranking of sites on the web:

"Page and Brin had clearly hit a nerve...with every person who labored over a website. To many, unleashing a ranking system, based on a bloodless algorithm, felt like a supreme act of arrogance. Who were these kids from Stanford telling the world how we ranked? What did they know about the work and the passion that went into our sites? Well, in truth, Page and Brim made no claim to such knowledge. As these early complaints illustrate, the Google service made no pretension about actually reading a particular site, or of understanding its content. It simply laid bare the often ugly truth of how well-connected a site happened to be. No matter how great a site might look or how many awards it might receive, if it was not linked to by other sites, ideally sites that were themselves well linked, then, in Google's estimation, it didn't really exist. That cold hard fact was hard for many to swallow."[134]

By mid 1998, Page and Brin sought out other search-oriented companies to license Google. At the time, they were reluctant to start their own company which might be swallowed up, or worse, smashed by the mega companies now positioning themselves on the web. They presented their technology to nearly every search-oriented company from Yahoo to Infoseek as well as several venture capitalists. Everyone thought their technology was interesting but no one could see how it could make money. These companies were all trying to create "portals" to the web: sites where people would come and stay not where people would be immediately hyperlinked away. Search was only the bait to bring people to their places of business. Most of these companies felt their search engines were good enough.

---

[134] John Battelle. *The Search.* Penguin Group Publishers, Sept. 8, 2005. 02:45:02 in the audible version.

Licensing Google was not going happen; starting their own company was the only way Google could find a home outside of Stanford. In an arranged meeting by a Stanford adviser, Brin and Page were introduced to Andy Bechtolsheim, one of the founders of Sun Microsystems,[135] who immediately saw Google's potential. Without any hesitation, he gave the inventors a cheque for $100,000 and said he would look in on them later. They didn't even know who he should make the cheque out to so he wrote it to Google Inc. This created a challenge as Google Inc. did not exist. They couldn't cash the cheque until, several weeks later, on September 7th, 1998, Google Inc. was incorporated with Page as CEO and Brin as President.

Google Inc. was launched out of a friend's garage and rented room in a five bedroom home. Through some other outside investment they were able to raise enough money to hire a few more engineering techs, but they quickly outgrew the garage. In the spring of 1999, the company relocated to an industrial complex in Palo Alto. As the Google index migrated from Stanford to their new complex, Google's insatiable appetite for processor time and storage space continued to grow. They perfected a means of linking inexpensive PC computers to combine the effort and storage.[136] And so the Google index grew and grew.

It was about this time that I remember my first search using Google. Being an Altavista user, I was a bit taken back by the almost blank page and simple graphic. But that first impression was set aside when I found what I was looking for on the top of the search results. I was looking for the Online Bible[137] (a new initiative to share free Bible software and resources over the internet) and there it was: number two on the Google listing. In other search engines this site was buried deep within commercial pages.

---

[135] www.sun.com One of the internet's most influential companies started by Stanford graduates. Sun created the UNIX workstation and Java script programming. Today they promote the best alternative for MS Office called OpenOffice which can be downloaded free at: http://www.openoffice.org/.
[136] This is called a server farm: http://en.wikipedia.org/wiki/Server_farm
[137] http://www.onlinebible.net

Even the Word of God was hard to find on the net at that time. I was immediately converted and to this day am an avid Google user. This book has been written with my browser poised at Google for the next search.

Eventually in June of 1999, Brin and Page found the real investment money to make Google into a viable internet company. Over the next two years, with an investment of multiple millions of dollars, their financiers began to require accountability and revenue from this new company. Larry and Sergey had to invite a new partner to their team, Eric E. Schmidt.

Schmidt was an engineering graduate of Princeton University, a successful executive from Sun Microsystems and had been CEO of Novell Networking from 1997 to 2001. Now he had to help Brin and Page become corporately acceptable and profitable. Not an easy task because of the anti-commercial, anti-advertising stance they had taken over the years. They began a compromise by adding Google AdWords. These Ads would not be allowed to change the culture they had built in this growing company. They adopted the motto: "do no evil."[138] They refused to give up the democratic way the software would answer a search query. The Ads would be listed on the side of the page and the advertiser would choose on which words they wanted to list their site. To this day Google is devoid of annoying banner ads and pop-ups. They seem to be staying true to their course.

Google now had a way to "make money without doing evil." And thus Google grew and grew and grew.

---

[138] Google. *Our Philosophy, Section 6.* Google Corporate Information. 5 April 2006. http://www.google.com/corporate/tenthings.html "**You can make money without doing evil.** Google is a business. The revenue the company generates is derived from offering its search technology to companies and from the sale of advertising displayed on Google and on other sites across the web. However, you may have never seen an ad on Google. That's because Google does not allow ads to be displayed on our results pages unless they're relevant to the results page on which they're shown. So, only certain searches produce sponsored links above or to the right of the results. Google firmly believes that ads can provide useful information if, and only if, they are relevant to what you wish to find."

By the summer of 2004, Google had secured a place in internet history. Larry Page and Sergey Brin had changed internet culture and made it realize that the future of search was indeed the future of the internet. That summer Google became a publicly traded company and by the end of year, tripled the value of its stocks. Page and Brin, in just a few short years, were launched to iconic status. They are now the "rock-stars" of the internet. Google continues to be the fastest growing company in digital history and some argue it will, in the next couple of years, pass the giants Microsoft, IBM and Intel as the digital world's most dominant technology.

Just Google It

Don't let the small and sudden beginnings of Google give you the idea that their ambitions are by any means insignificant. Larry and Sergey have entered into a world that only a few others in history have come. They are now among the ranks of inventors like Gutenberg, Joseph Henry, Henry Morse, Alexander Bell and Bill Gates (who is really a marketing genius, not an inventor, but his name sounds cool in this list). They are listed in the top 25 richest men in the world. They have big plans for their wealth.

On Google's Corporate Information Webpage the bold statement announces their intentions:

"Google's mission is to organize the world's information and make it universally accessible and useful."[139]

Organize the what? The world's information?! Can this be possible? So far they are on track. They have had to overcome hurdles, particularly anyone who publishes intellectual property but does not want it freely accessible by Google, but even this is changing in the new world of "net-ethics." Google has developed a number of partnerships

---

[139] Google. *Company Overview.* Google Corporate Information. 5 April 2006. http://www.google.com/corporate/

with libraries, universities and information services to digitalize any and all text in the world, that's right, everything in the world, from the Harvard Classics to what is written on cereal boxes. Its insatiable appetite to gather, index, know and distribute continues to grow at a faster rate than Microsoft did when it gobbled up any and all companies it its wake.

In five short years Google is a cultural icon. The phrase "just Google it" is applied to anything we need to know. It is not uncommon to hear someone say "I googled that article" or "I googled my term paper," or how about, "I googled your name and found..." Even if we use another search engine, we still say "I googled it at Yahoo." You have a part in the digital world when you know what that phrase means.

Something has changed in the psyche of our culture. I can't recall exactly when I started to experience this change in my consciousness of knowledge. Perhaps it began when I discovered Google or maybe a bit later as I honed my search techniques. My conscious concern for knowledge, or rather my lack thereof, shifted to a sense of security, a false sense I might add, that I could find nearly anything I need to know on the net. Thanks to Google, I knew where and how to start my learning acquisition. This is a dangerous thing for a fellow who makes his living as an educator. This new consciousness is the reason I titled this chapter, "Informational**ism**." There is something deeper happening to our culture. Information is becoming an "ism," a religion with its own set of morals and ethics. If something can be known, then it is immoral to not be able to find it. People are worshiping everyday at the computer screens of this new religion. Google is the temple and Brin and Page are the high priests.

Google is causing me rethink how we educate our children and young people. Do we concentrate our focus on teaching "facts" that can easily be googled at any time or place, or should we focus our attention on teaching our students how to search? I am a huge advocate for good, scholarly research and getting the facts right. Certainly, the teacher must "give the facts." But in an age where any and every fact is right there, literally at their fingertips, is it not more important for us to teach how to find the right facts, and when these are found, how to critically think about them? Teaching our kids how to search will become one of the compulsory topics of education.

Google is changing how we do business. It has become my first choice when I need to find a product or vender. I like the democratic approach of being able to choose based on Google's criteria rather than on good marketing savvy. There are still a few flaws as Google can still be partially manipulated by those who try to beat PageRank. But generally, I can find almost anything I want by just "googling it."

Google Is Watching You

I have personally been googled recently. I was contacted by three different people from my past, twenty-six years in my past. Two of my former US Navy shipmates typed "Greg Bitgood" into the search engine and my name appeared exclusively on the first three pages of links. Obviously, my name appeared because of my publications on the web and my involvement with an online school. What was very encouraging to me was that both of these gentlemen remembered my Christian witness during our time in the service. Both made contact through email and one sent a prophecy that was very encouraging. The other contact was a friend who was involved in a Bible Study we attended together back in my Navy days.

Typing your own name into Google is typically called an "ego-search." It is always amusing to see if you are "web-famous" and hearing from old friends can be very rewarding, but there is also a dark side to this type of search.

Consider the fact that Google doesn't rank your search by the date. What if a negative article was written in your local newspaper or company newsletter? As long as it stays on the web and Google's crawlers find it, your name will live in infamy. Keep in mind that Google isn't the only way you can be immortalized on the web. Perhaps a student or a coworker decides to name you in a blog. In most cases blogs are personal diaries containing the subjective opinions of those who post and who have enough gumption to write about you for others to see. This opinion will stay in the search zone for as long as it sits on the web. A quick search of a name at Technorati.com[140] can yield some surprising results. As internet searches continue to expand to include more and more digital documentation, it is only a matter of time before more our life history is digitalized.

There is no more powerful search than that of yourself. Such was the case of Orie Steinman, a 17 year old boy living with his mother. When he googled his name, he discovered that he had been abducted by his mother in an ugly custody battle 15 years earlier. She had fled Ontario, Canada and relocated in California. Orie discovered that his father had been looking for him ever since she had taken him out of the country. He told his school teacher, his mother was arrested and he was reunited with his father.

Anyone who works in a personnel oriented occupation can now use Google to find out information about people. Are you going to hire that executive? Check their job history. Are you going on a date, or is your daughter? Google the family name, there is no telling what you might learn - he might be wanted by the F.B.I. One gal in New York did just that: she googled her blind date's name and he came up on the FBI wanted list. She alerted the authorities and he was captured.

What will happen when someone is not found in the index? Are they in a lower class or so mysterious that they have avoided the Google crawlers? What conclusions will we make of someone we can't google. Are they really who they say they are? Do they really exist? In this age of information, it will be very difficult to hide.

As Christians, what should we do with such information? What happens when someone's life before they be-

---

[140] http://www.technorati.com/ At the time of this writing, this blog site search engine was tracking 32.1 million sites with over 2.2 billion links.

came a Christian comes back to haunt them? Just recently I have had to deal with a situation in a friend's life where he was involved in a sexual sin almost fifteen years ago while in his first ministry assignment. When this information was recently unearthed, his blunder came back to haunt him. It has cost him his current position and possibly his ministry. He had undergone a thorough restoration with the ministry he was under and worked everything out with his own family, but this was not included in the information. Because he did not disclose this issue in his current employment, he was immediately fired. If something stays on the internet, it will be in the index. The Google algorithm doesn't care when it was posted. Google doesn't forgive, nor does it forget.

Google Morality

Sergey Brin and Larry Page have been placed in the untenable role of making moral decisions that have the potential to shape our entire culture. They have begun to ban certain types of searches. Don't get rid of your content blocker yet, they typically block sites devoted to racial hate. Mostly they refuse to allow them to advertise, but it is very difficult to completely block the links from the search window. At this point, Google and most other search engines have no intention of blocking pornography. It is still very profitable for the search engines. Google and other search engines will help you set up a personal profile that can filter most pornographic sites in your searches; you have to personally enable this feature. The content blocking program[141] that our family uses does this for us and blocks access to changing the settings.

Recently, Google has come under criticism because it had to review its policy of censoring sites in order to gain access into China. The Chinese government has been busy

---

[141] http://www.contentwatch.com/ We like this particular product because of the multiple features. It allows you to set up various profiles for multiple users and stores on the internet.

during the last couple of years, with some very interesting partners such as Microsoft and IBM, building what many internet journalists call "the great firewall of China." The bamboo curtain has never really fallen; it has only given us a chance to squeeze through the slats. This is not what Chinese officials are saying, though. In an interview with the Evangelical Alliance staff, one official felt free enough to use the phrase "bamboo curtain:"

"China's ambassador to Australia, Madame Fu Ying publicly denied Chen's remarks saying, 'China has moved on a long way from what it was like in the 1970s. China is not a country behind the bamboo curtain any more.'"[142]

The curtain is probably translucent when it comes to the internet but there are still millions of blocked sites in China. Google has publicly admitted their compromise on the company's official blog:

"Filtering our search results clearly compromises our mission. Failing to offer Google search at all to a fifth of the world's population, however, does so far more severely. Whether our critics agree with our decision or not, due to the severe quality problems faced by users trying to access Google.com from within China, this is precisely the choice we believe we faced. By launching Google.cn and making a major ongoing investment in people and infrastructure within China, we intend to change that."[143]

An interesting note: the "Digital Bible Society" website, my brother's ministry that was featured in the chapter

---

[142] Elizabeth Kendal. *China's Bamboo Curtain*. World Evangelical Alliance Religious Liberty News & Analysis. Friday 24 June 2005 http://www.evangelicalalliance.org.au/rlc/WEADetail.php?ID=497
[143] Andrew McLaughlin. *Google in China*. Google Blog, 27 January 2006 11:58 http://googleblog.blogspot.com/2006/01/google-in-china.html This is the official cooperate blog for Google.

on Globalization,[144]is banned in China. Ken indicated that it was probably due to the information the site provides on Chinese citizens presently under persecution and not because of the Bible content. They are working on a site which will feature the Bible software that might make it through the bamboo slats.

Knowledge Puffs Up

We are faced with a world that, in the near future, will believe that all knowledge is now available, at least everything that is presently known. But having knowledge of a thing can still be very deceptive. Dietrich Bonhoeffer, the great German martyr of World War II, is helpful in articulating the contrast between knowledge and wisdom:

"To understand reality is not the same as to know about outward events. It is to perceive the essential nature of things. The best-informed man is not necessarily the wisest. Indeed there is a danger that precisely in the multiplicity of his knowledge he will lose sight of what is essential. But on the other hand, knowledge of an apparently trivial detail quite often makes it possible to see into the depth of things. And so the wise man will seek to acquire the best possible knowledge about events, but always without becoming dependent upon this knowledge. To recognize the significant in the factual is wisdom."[145]

---

[144] Pages 109-112 in the section "Who Is My Neighbor?"

[145] *Wisdom Quotations*. 5 April 2006
http://www.wisdomquotes.com/cat_wisdom.html I have become the victim of the very thing I am writing about. By searching Google for quotes on "wisdom versus knowledge", I found this wonderful quote by the great Bonhoeffer. What I could not find after an hour of searching was the reference to this quote. I have several of his books but, alas, I was unable to locate this great quote which is definitely vintage Bonhoeffer. I ask anyone who might be reading this to please send me the original source and I will put it in the next printing. This has provided a good illustration of one of the current problems with the internet.

If we become dependent upon the internet to the exclusion of finding God's context for any given knowledge, we will find ourselves on dangerous ground. The scriptures are quite clear about this danger:

> *If I have the gift of prophecy and can fathom all mysteries and all knowledge, and if I have a faith that can move mountains, but have not love, I am nothing.*
> I Corinthians 13:2 (NIV)

> *...We sometimes tend to think we know all we need to know to answer these kinds of questions-- but sometimes our humble hearts can help us more than our proud minds. We never really know enough until we recognize that God alone knows it all.*
> I Corinthians 8:1b-3 (The Message) [146]

These statements from the Word of God help us see that knowledge or information is not the answer to the world's needs. It comes back to trust in God who really knows everything.

As Christians we have to remember that our true source of knowledge is in God first and anything beyond Him must be superintended by the Spirit of Truth.[147] The question should never be about information, it should be about truth. Neil Postman sounds like the ancient prophet as he warns us in *Technopoly* about the "ism" of faith in Information alone:

> "But the genie that came out of the bottle proclaiming that information was the new god of culture was a deceiver. It solved the problem of information scarcity,

---

[146] (NIV) New International Version and The Message Version can both be found at http://www.biblegateway.com. This site is where I find most of my Bible references. About a year ago I found that I was doing more research online than in my resident computer program.
[147] John 16:13 (NIV) *But when he, the Spirit of truth, comes, he will guide you into all truth...*

the disadvantages of which were obvious. But it gave no warning about the dangers of information glut, the disadvantages of which were not seen so clearly. The long-range result - information chaos - has produced a culture somewhat like the shuffled deck of cards I referred to. And what is strange is that so few have noticed, or if they have noticed fail to recognize the source of their distress."[148]

The internet is becoming our library for human knowledge. Many of my educational colleagues are often suspicious of the internet when used as a source for knowledge and I say, rightly so. But if they point our students to public libraries, I would suggest that this is just as precarious as finding research on Google. In fact, the internet is making our students look much more "scholarly" in their reports and essays by citing this paper and that quote, just as I have done in this book. In many cases, internet research is giving rise to plagiarism. Thankfully, the searchable web addresses this issue as well. Take any suspected plagiarized document and insert a paragraph of it into Google - up pops the references. There are sites dedicated to finding these intellectual thieves among us such as, Plagerism.org.[149]

The readiness of digital information has introduced us to the world of intellectual property rights. The ease with which we can transfer information in its various formats has created an entire industry for taking advantage of those rights. Most of us remember the Napster[150] controversy. In 1999, college student Shawn Fanning, wrote an internet application that made it easy for peer-to-peer file sharing.[151] He made it possible to grab files off your com-

---

[148] Neil Postman, *Technopoly: The Surrender of Culture to Technology*, New York, Vintage Books, 1993 page 60
[149] This site links to software, such as *Turnitin* and *iThenticat* that educators can use to discovering plagiarism.
[150] http://en.wikipedia.org/wiki/Napster
[151] Peer-to-peer means any computer to any computer that is networked. No server is necessary for the activity.

puter and share them with anyone else using Napster. The primary file sharing activity was digitalized music. "You can copy my songs if I can copy your songs," was the idea. Napster drew the attention of the music industry and incurred several lawsuits. This eventually meant that Napster was sued for millions of dollars and shut down. In September of 2001, to somehow pay these costs, they tried to set up a subscription service that went nowhere. Today, there are several underground Napster-like programs on the web transferring terabytes of files.

The battle is raging to control intellectual property on the web. What is really changing is our fundamental respect for the idea of intellectual property rights. The ease of access to information has meant that the rights to such information and content are not highly valued. "Thou shalt not steal"[152] doesn't seem to apply here. A new ethic is emerging that is changing how we think about information in general: if it can be digitized, then it should be shared. The Christian youth I work with in our schools and church have adopted this new ethic, unless, of course, they have become successful musicians.

The Google-searchable world is full of new challenges in every area of our lives. It is the new ideas about knowledge that may prove to be the most challenging aspects of our future.

We must answer the questions that Informationalism brings, before it is to late.

- Is having access to knowledge and information too much?
- Do we trust the new Google morality?
- Do we trust what we find on Google?
- What type of information should be disclosed and what type should be kept private?
- Do we believe in the boundaries of "intellectual property rights"?

---

[152] Exodus 20:15 (KJV)

- Is it wrong to download and share music, movies, books and other copyright media?
- Are we teaching our children how and what to search for on this vast landscape of human information?
- Are we developing critical thinking skills that can decipher the truth from fantasy, the real from the false?
- Have we grounded our young people in the true Source of knowledge?
- How well are we discipling this generation in the Word of God?
- When they walk the hallways of this immense library of human information, do they acknowledge and follow the presence of the Spirit of Truth?
- Do we know how to consult and search the only infinite, omniscient mind of God?

Thanks to Larry and Sergey, we may be behind the times concerning some of these questions. I propose we put our WWJG stickers and wristbands on our computer monitors, our screen savers and our foreheads. Perhaps the most important question today is "What Would Jesus Google?"

Biotechnology

My mind was filled with one thought, one conception, one
purpose. So much has been done, exclaimed the soul of
Frankenstein—more, far more, will I achieve; treading in
the steps already marked, I will pioneer a new way, explore
unknown powers, and unfold to the world the deepest mys-
teries of creation.

Dr. Victor Frankenstein[153]

Mary was only sixteen when she ran away with Percy Shelley. He was in his early twenties but had already had one failed marriage. He fashioned himself a political radical and free thinker. Percy would shortly be discovered as an up-and-coming author and poet. By the time Mary was nineteen, she was becoming somewhat disillusioned with her life. Percy and Mary traveled to Lake Geneva for a summer holiday but were forced to stay indoors because of an unusually cold and rainy summer. After a night of visiting with fellow artisans and intellectuals, Mary had one of those strange experiences that happen just before one falls asleep; she had a waking dream. She describes her vision:

---

[153] Mary Shelley. *Frankenstein*. Heritage Christian School Classics publication. Chapter 3, Page 24. Like any classic that is older than 75 years, it can be downloaded and reprinted. I recommend www.clasicreader.com .

"...with shut eyes, but acute mental vision—I saw the pale student of unhallowed arts kneeling beside the thing he had put together. I saw the hideous phantasm of a man stretched out, and then, on the working of some powerful engine, show signs of life and stir with an uneasy, half-vital motion. Frightful must it be, for supremely frightful would be the effect of any human endeavor to mock the stupendous mechanism of the Creator of the world...."[154]

Immediately, she began to write one of the most important classics of her time, *Frankenstein*. The book was published in 1817 at a time when Science was taking hold of its new hallowed place in our culture. Mary would publish one more book in her lifetime, a science fiction novel called *The Last Man,* but its success was limited. Her husband died a few years later in a drowning accident and Mary devoted the rest of her life to editing and publishing his works.

Several summers ago, I downloaded and reprinted the book. I made it required reading for the Bitgood teenagers. My four children have a strong propensity for science and mathematics and I felt this would be a great book for discussions around our dinner table. It was an interesting but scary summer. Yes, the monster is terrifying but not for the reasons you think. If all you know about the story is what you have seen in Hollywood movies you will miss this point. What makes the story so frightening is how easily we can identify with Victor Frankenstein.

The story of Dr. Frankenstein should warn us of what a mind driven toward scientific understanding and creation is capable of. The young doctor's driven nature and his drive toward science put all questions of ethics and morality out of his mind. You can hear his regret for his lack of circumspection:

---

[154] Mary Shelley. *Frankenstein*. Preface, 1831 edition. This quote describes the vision that inspired the novel and the prototypes for Victor Frankenstein and his monster.

"For this I had deprived myself of rest and health. I had desired it with an ardor that far exceeded moderation; but now that I had finished, the beauty of the dream vanished, and breathless horror and disgust filled my heart."[155]

He created a monster because the science of the thing drove him to it. He did it just because it was possible.

Biology + Digital World = Biotechnology

Your body is digital. Electronic signals are coursing through your entire body as you read this book. Your eyes are sending an analog picture, captured by 130 million receptors, to your brain through electric signals carried by the optic nerve.[156] These signals are going to the occipital lobe[157] at the back of the brain. This is your visual processing center. The digital signal carried by the nerves makes contact with tissues of the brain and chemically transfers the information. Your brain then sees these signals and sends the information to millions of other interpretive centers. Mix in some magic, zap it here and there and, voila, you are reading this page!

As our technology becomes predominately digital, we have opportunities to merge the engineering sciences with the life sciences. The marriage of the body and machine is now possible through translating these digital signals. The biological sciences are becoming the new frontier for digital research.

In the essay, *The Merger of Flesh and Machines* written for the futuristic book: *The Next Fifty Years: Science in the First Half of the Twenty-First Century*, Rodney

---

[155] Mary Shelley. *Frankenstein*. Heritage Christian School Classics publication. Chapter 5, page 31
[156] http://en.wikipedia.org/wiki/Optic_nerves 3 April 2006
[157] http://en.wikipedia.org/wiki/Occipital_lobe 3 April 2006

Brooks[158] writes about the changes taking place in the sciences. He is a leading scientist in this field.

"Fifty years ago, just after the Second World War, there was a transformation of engineering. Before that engineering had been a craft based exercise. But starting around 1950, it was transformed into a physics based discipline. Now we are seeing the beginnings of a transformation of engineering again. This time into a largely biologically based discipline, though it will not sacrifice the rigor of its physics background. At MIT's Artificial Intelligence Laboratory where I am director, I see signs of this transformation every day. We have torn out clean rooms where we used to make silicon chips and installed wet labs in their place, where we compile programs into DNA sequences that we splice into genomes in order to breed bacterial robots. Our thirty year goal is to have such exquisite control over the genetics of living systems that instead of growing a tree, cutting it down and building a table out of it. We will ultimately be able to grow the table. We have turned labs where we used to assemble silicon and steel robots into labs where we assemble robots from silicon, steel and living cells." [159]

What is happening at MIT is not unusual. Until recently, technology has mostly been a means for extending ourselves into our environment. We have focused on transportation technologies that have taken us to other planets.

---

[158] http://people.csail.mit.edu/brooks/ Rodney Brooks is Director of the MIT Computer Science and Artificial Intelligence Laboratory, and is the Panasonic Professor of Robotics. He is also Chief Technical Officer of iRobot Corp (nasdaq: IRBT). He received a degree in pure mathematics from the Flinders University of South Australia and his Ph.D. in Computer Science from Stanford University in 1981. His views are considered very "naturalistic." In the quoted article he explicitly states that "man is a machine" and "there is no soul."

[159] John Brockman, ed. *The Next Fifty Years: Science in the First Half of the Twenty-First Century.* Brooks, R.A. *The Merger of Flesh and Machines.* Vintage Books-Randomhouse, Inc., 2002. Pages 183–193.

We have networked trillions of kilometers of fiber optics so that a phone call from Bangalore, India sounds like it came from next door. But science is now looking for ways to get smaller so that we can join technology to the human experience. In the book *Radical Evolution,* Joel Garreau addresses this shift in priorities.

> "For all previous millennia, our technologies have been aimed outward, to control our environment.... Now, however, we have started a wholesale process of aiming our technologies inward. Now our technologies have started to merge with our minds, our memories, our metabolisms, our personalities, our progeny and perhaps our souls. Serious people have embarked on changing humans so much that they call it a new kind of engineered evolution – one that we direct for ourselves."[160]

Note that last phrase "a new kind of engineered evolution." With the naturalistic worldview of evolution it is no wonder that science is beginning to move in this direction. I have watched many an episode of *Star Trek* that proposed this idea. Mankind's merge with technology would push us further in our evolutionary ascent as a species. This continues to present some of the most serious questions the human race has been faced with, the biggest being: *"What is man that you are mindful of him?"* Psalm 8:4 (NIV) Rodney Brooks continues in his essay, *The Merger of Flesh and Machines,* to ask these very same questions. Brooks writes,

> "...there will be an alteration in our view of ourselves as a species. We will begin to see ourselves as simply a part of the infrastructure of industry. While all the scientific and technical work proceeds we will again and again be confronted with the same constellations of disturbing questions. What is it to be alive? What

---

[160] Joel Garreau. *Radical Evolution: The Promise and Peril of Enhancing Our Minds, Our Bodies -- and What It Means to Be Human.* P. Doubleday, May 2005. Page 6.

makes something human? What makes something sub-human? What is a Super-human? What changes can we accept in humanity? Is it ethical to manipulate human life? Is it ethical to manipulate human life in particular corrective ways? Whose version of corrective? Whose version of life and human? What responsibility does the individual scientist have for whatever forms of life he or she may manipulate or create? And these questions will not only be asked in the well meaning precincts of science, they will be thrashed out in the larger society accompanied by everything from vandalism to terrorism to full fledged war."[161]

The stark difference between Brooks and the Psalmist of scripture is that Brooks seeks the answer from human reason and rejects the wisdom of the Creator God. By rejecting God's wisdom he has only himself and other scientists to find the answers to these enormous questions. He is correct in predicting great conflict over these essential questions. The directions that we take in these new sciences could be very different depending on if we answer these questions from a religious point of view versus a scientific point of view.

Scientists know what is at stake here. This may be the deeper reason why many scientists and science organizations are fighting the teaching of *Intelligent Design*[162] in our public schools. They know that if the world was created by an intelligent mind, then there are ethical issues that must be addressed in the sciences. The Creator would have something to say about the way we are mucking about in His creation and how we are manipulating it.

---

[161] John Brockman, ed. *The Next Fifty Years: Science in the First Half of the Twenty-First Century.* Brooks, R.A. *The Merger of Flesh and Machines.* Vintage Books-Randomhouse, Inc., 2002. Pages 183–193.

[162] The Intelligent Design Movement is a non-religious attempt to challenge Darwinism in modern scientific circles and present scientific evidence that the Universe could have been created by an Intelligent Mind. A good place to learn more about ID is at the Access Research Network website: http://www.arn.org/

This line of thought calls to mind a funny story:

All of the scientists of the world gathered together in a great conference and decided they were advanced to the point that they could challenge God. They called Him to a contest of wits.

"Almighty God, you have done well with creation to this point but we don't need You anymore," stated the spokesperson.

"Really," replied God. "What do you propose?"

"We propose to create life - and not just any life; we will make a sophisticated life form out of non-life!"

"Well, that's pretty good," said God. "I can't wait to see what you come up with."

The scientists began gathering the raw materials they would use to build their creation when they were suddenly interrupted by God.

"Wait a minute guys, who said you could use my dirt?"

Mapping the Human Genome

"On February 28, 1953, Francis Crick walked into the Eagle Pub in Cambridge, England, …and announced that, 'we had found the secret of life.'"[163] Earlier that day, Francis Crick and James Watson had seen the structure of deoxyribonucleic acid, DNA in an x-ray. This "double helix" confirmed suspicions that DNA carries life's hereditary information. Years later, these two scientists received the Nobel Prize for their discovery of the building blocks of life. Watson eventually became the head of the Human Genome Project.

Another "Aha!" moment came fifty years later. In a thirteen year project, funded by the US Department of Energy and the National Institutes of Health, the "Human

---

[163] Robert Wright. *James Watson & Francis Crick. The Time 100: The Most Important People of the Century* 29 March 1999. © 2003 Time Inc.
http://www.time.com/time/time100/scientist/profile/watsoncrick.html

Genome Project"[164] announced that they had successfully mapped the human DNA molecule. This meant that they identified all 25,000 genes in human DNA. They also sequenced the 3,000,000,000 chemical base pairs in the DNA. They have put all of this information into databases and made it available for public research.

DNA is the digital signature of God's hand upon creation. Dr. Francis S. Collins is the Director of the National Human Genome Research Institute in Bethesda, Maryland. He is also a passionate Christian. In an article written for *The Center For Bioethics and Human Dignity* he talks about God's wonderful design in DNA.

"To understand hereditary factors, we must understand the wonderful molecule called DNA, the double helical structure of which Watson and Crick figured out some forty-seven years ago. It is a very elegant system of encoding information. What a privilege it is for a physician-scientist to do research that uncovers something about our creation and gives us a glimpse into the elegant way God thinks! DNA is certainly a remarkable way of coding information in a very efficient, elegant and digital fashion, allowing us to carry around an enormous amount of information in a very modest space."[165]

The work on the human genome is beginning to yield some amazing breakthroughs in medicine. Scientists have isolated many of the genetic causes of diseases such as breast cancer, Alzheimer's disease, leukemia, cystic fibrosis and many others. By narrowing down this information, it will help speed the production of medicines and cures.

---

[164] http://www.ornl.gov/sci/techresources/Human_Genome/home.shtml
[165] Francis S. Collins, MD, PhD. *Reflections from the Director of the National Human Genome Research Institute.* The Center for Bioethics and Human Dignity. Copyright 2001. Collins is the Director of the National Human Genome Research Institute in Bethesda, Maryland.
http://www.cbhd.org/resources/genetics/collins_2001-07-06.htm

This new breakthrough in science can be a wonderful thing to help relieve human suffering, speed our healing abilities and ultimately, prolong life. But can this knowledge be used in other ways? Is it possible to engineer a better human being?

It would be hard to find someone to argue the morality of helping those who are injured, deformed or diseased with new medical breakthroughs. But consider those who use medical or genetic solutions to enhance their abilities in order to perform above the norm.

Enhancing the human experience with metabolic and surgical means is not a new thing. We have been enhancing humans with steroids so they can run faster, hit further and jump higher. We have been helping 55-year-old men perform in the bedroom like 25-year-old men. We have been altering female anatomy in ways that make women more socially appealing.

There are significant differences between using a scalpel to alter one's body and sequencing, splicing and altering one's genetics to bring about the desired enhancement.

Enhancing the Species

First, we need to understand that there are two types of genetic engineering.[166]

---

[166] My research in genetics, a topic admittedly I've know very little about until this project, was at the following websites:

o *Wikipedia - Gene Therapy.* http://en.wikipedia.org/wiki/Gene_therapy ;
o *Wikipedia - The Human Genome Project.*
   http://en.wikipedia.org/wiki/Human_Genome_Project
o *The Center for Bioethics and Human Dignity* – section on Genetics
   .http://www.cbhd.org/resources/genetics/index.html
o *The National Human Genome Research Institute*
   http://www.genome.gov/
o Joel Garreau. *Radical Evolution: The Promise and Peril of Enhancing our Minds, our Bodies-and what it means to be Human.* Random House, 2005

Somatic gene engineering works to fix genes within a single person's body. This type of gene therapy can be done inside the body or, cells can be removed, the genes spliced and altered and then returned to the body. This type of genetic manipulation is not very controversial except when it brings harm to the patient. Most current genetic research has been focused on this type of therapy and can be thought of in the same way as surgery.

The second type of genetic engineering, which poses the greatest potential to alter our very humanity, is called Germ-line genetics. Germ-line engineering alters the genetic makeup at the very beginning of human life. Genetic manipulation is introduced to an embryo and affects every cell that reproduces itself from this tiny human being. Beyond the affects in that one person, this alteration will be carried on in their children, grandchildren and propagated to all of their descendants.

Suppose we are able to alter human genetics so that we can make stronger, faster or taller people. What if this genetic mutation continues to advance itself in future generations? We would eventually have a race of people with, compared to us today, superhuman powers. Suppose we are able to do the same with intelligence and memory. We would eventually have a race of super brilliant people. Would these people be considered better than the rest of humanity or would they be discriminated against based on their genetics?

Genetic mutation and manipulation is becoming a popular topic in today's film industry. It is the premise of the comic book series and major block buster movies, *X-Men*. The mutants in *X-men* are discriminated against because society fears their abilities. The mutants are exiled and go in two opposing directions. One group resents the non-genetically enhanced society's rejection of their gifts and plots to take over the world, while another group dedicates themselves to protect the non-genetically enhanced populations of the world. The 1997 film, *Gattica,* suggests that discrimination will go to the other extreme. Only those with genetically enhanced minds and bodies are allowed to be involved in the important aspects of society. Those who are naturally born, without any genetic enhancement, are considered sub-human.

These ideas presuppose that we are able to alter our genetics in this fashion. In a practical reality, we are still a long way away from real significant alterations. Genetic manipulation could turn out to be much more difficult in humans than has been portrayed by those who request the research money to press forward. Scientists have altered mice in certain ways to create what they call "super mice." For example, researchers have engineered "marathon mice" which can run without fatigue twice as long as a normal mouse. In addition, "Schwarzenegger mice" are named for their bulked up muscles when specific genetic alterations are made in their muscle tissue. In a CBS News article, researcher Dr. Ronald Evans of Salk Institute in San Diego commented on his mice,[167] "The enhanced performance of the mouse could translate into human athleticism," Evans said. When asked if this research was being tested in humans, Evan's commented, "There's a big gulf between mice and men, and the field of gene therapy has yielded mixed results over the last decade, including the death of a human subject five years ago."[168] He is referring to the widely publicized death of Jesse Gelsinger in 1999, the subject of a gene therapy trial.

One of the biggest ethical issues in genetics is the limited ability to predict certain diseases and problems when life is at its earliest stages. This could create similar problems as determining the sex of a baby in the womb has. Millions of abortions around the world have been performed simply because the child was not the right gender. Consider that we can predict certain birth defects in developing embryos and then select which embryos to be implanted in the mother and allowed to live.

---

[167] *Gene-Alteration Makes Super Mice.* SAN FRANCISCO. The Associated Press, 24 August 2004 ©MMIV
http://www.cbsnews.com/stories/2004/08/24/tech/main637939.shtml
[168] Ibid.

Note the word "embryo." This is the term used for a fertilized egg in the early stages of development: the first five to eight weeks. When I came to the Wikipedia article on *embryo*, I found a problem with the definition that reflects the typical approach toward human life. Here is the original quote:

"Description: In organisms that reproduce sexually, once a sperm fertilizes an egg cell, the result is a cell called the zygote that has all the DNA of two parents. In plants, animals, and some protists, the zygote will begin to divide by mitosis to produce a multicellular organism. The term embryo refers to the early stages of this development, after the zygote has divided at least once, but before the process has completed to produce an individual."[169]

I went ahead and edited this entry to read "the next stage of development," which is still part of the article thus far. The original author made the common mistake of assigning personhood to one stage in human development. Of course this unearths the common arguments against abortion. Life begins at conception, not when the embryo fastens itself to the mother's uterus, not when a certain organ develops, not when brain function is recognizable, not when we change the name of the stage of development from embryo to fetus and not when the baby in the womb gets an address change and lives outside of the mom! Life begins when the sperm enters the egg and a brand-new genetic-information-set is established. We have the same 46 chromosomes[170] today as we did at the miracle of our conception.

---

[169] *Embryo.* Wikipedia, The Free Encyclopedia. 29 March 2006 23:15 UTC http://en.wikipedia.org/wiki/Embryo

[170] "The DNA which carries genetic information in cells is normally packaged in the form of one or more large macromolecules called chromosomes." *Chromosome.* Wikipedia, the Free Encyclopedia. 5 April 2006 18:20 UTC http://en.wikipedia.org/wiki/Chromosomes

Here is the dark and sinister reality of what is happening. Each embryo is a human being. When a doctor implants the sperm into the egg via the test tube, he is facilitating the conception of a unique, individual life. In order to successfully make a genetic comparison, multiple human lives will begin only to end in destruction.

A 2004 article in USA Today[171] told the story of an Irish family trying to solve a rare genetic disease in their son, Joshua, known as "Diamond-Blackfan anemia." When he reaches puberty, his body will lack the ability to produce red blood cells. His parents hope to solve his condition by giving him a stem cell transplant. Unfortunately, Joshua's brother is not a compatible donor. His parents are attempting to gain stem cells from their embryos. Doctors are fertilizing his mother's eggs with his father's sperm to create multiple "embryos" in the hope that one of these will become an adequate stem cell donor for Joshua. When compatible embryos are discovered, they will be implanted into mom. When his sibling is born, the stem cells from the newborn's umbilical cord will be transplanted into Joshua's liver and he will stand a very good chance of completely beating this disease. This all sounds heroic, except, what about the dozens of Joshua's brothers and sisters who will be killed in the process of finding a cure? Samuel D. Hensley, MD, is Fellow of The Center for Bioethics and Human Dignity and a Surgical Pathologist; he comments on this very case in his article, *Designer Babies: One Step Closer.*

"This procedure is illegal in Great Britain and is regarded as unethical. Why? Before exploring the British objection, let me add an additional concern from a Christian perspective that regards these embryos as early human life, made in the image of God, possessing unique genes and the capability of continued hu-

---

[171] Rita Rubin. *Health and Behavior: Early genetic testing allays fears, ignites ethics debate.* USA TODAY 26 May 2004
http://www.usatoday.com/news/health/2004-05-26-stemcell-testing-usat_x.htm

man development. An important question for Christians is what will happen to the healthy embryos that are incompatible with Joshua. Will they be implanted later and given an equal chance at continued life or will they be discarded? Embryos not selected may be destroyed directly or by destructive embryo research, which is contrary to an understanding of human life being sacred. The USA Today article does not mention what plans the parents have for these other offspring."[172]

The multiple ethical and moral issues just on the horizon in the field of genetics will prove to be some of the trickiest waters the church will have to navigate. One interesting voice in the debate has been Dr. Bernard Nathanson. You might remember him as the doctor who shocked the world with the video, *The Silent Scream*. It was an ultrasound video recorded during an actual abortion with Nathanson's commentary. I will never forget the image at the beginning of the procedure when you can clearly make out the painful expression of the baby. Nathanson eventually stopped performing abortions and, after witnessing the relentless testimony of pro-lifers, gave his life to Christ in 1997. On February 9th, 2000 he was asked to address the US Congress on Reproductive Technologies. Here is an excerpt from his address:

"The manipulation of human beings seems to have no limits. This technology threatens the human species far more than abortion does. Abortion is a one-on-one destruction of a human being. What I am talking about today is a totality of changing the human species in defining what we are as humans.... We're looking at somatic immortality on this planet in the next 100 years.... The geneticists, in short, are running wild. I am demanding Congress get involved in this to

---

[172] Samuel D. Hensley. *Designer Babies: One Step Closer,* The Center for Bioethics and Human Dignity – Genetics. 1 July 2004
http://www.cbhd.org/resources/genetics/hensley_2004-07-01.htm

a much greater extent than it already has. We are looking at the same problem we had with nuclear power. In 1945, we dropped two bombs on Hiroshima and Nagasaki then spent the next 50 years arguing the ethics of it. We chased that horse down the street after the barn door was already locked."[173]

Mapping the human genome is the beginning of where the digital world finds its way into the very building blocks of life. It took thirteen years and twelve billion dollars to accomplish. In ten years from now it will cost less than twelve dollars to map your own DNA. You will be able to walk into a clinic, give your physician a password and your entire genetic information will be at his disposal. Just think, we will be able to google you in ways you never imagined.

The Stem Cell Debate

In July 2004, Kim Lewis woke up in hard labor; she had been pregnant with the twins for 27 weeks. Her husband, Adam, rushed her to the hospital where she gave birth to Sam and Katie. Though they were born prematurely, both are healthy. What makes these two babies different is that just seven months earlier they were taken from a bank of frozen embryos in an infertility clinic. These two six-month-old babies could actually be many more years old depending upon when they were created and how long they were frozen. Kim and Adam are now very happy parents.

Kim: "I am so thankful for those years of infertility. If I had been able to get pregnant on my own, we would not have had Katie and Sam. I have an appreciation for these beautiful babies that I would never have

---

[173] Dr. Bernard Nathanson. *Ethical Considerations: Bernard Nathanson Testifies Before Congress on Reproductive Technologies.* 9 February 2000. From the pro-life website: http://www.marianland.com/nathanson001.html

had. These children will not have a chance to live unless someone carries them."

Adam: "We have seen the goodness of God through this. There is hope through embryo adoption. It opens up a whole new door for infertility. The embryos are genetically separate, living beings with the ability to grow. They are life. Katie and Sam are proof of that."[174]

Stem cells have become the latest controversy in the biotechnical world because many scientists are insisting on using human embryonic stem cells for their research. They fertilize multiple human eggs with sperm to start the first stage of human life.

A stem cell is unique because it is a builder cell. Stem cells divide and become other cells. There are three basic types of stem cells. Totipotent stem cells have total potential. When an embryonic stem cell divides, each daughter cell becomes either another stem cell or any other cell in the body. The DNA in the stem cell has encoded within it the ability to become a muscle, brain tissue, blood or any other cell of the body.

Adults continue to produce stem cells called multipotent (multiple potential), and unipotent (one potential). Adult stem cells are only able to divide into the closely related family of cells they came from.

One of the most promising places to find stem cells is in the umbilical cord, known as cord blood stem cells. There are umbilical cord blood banks in almost every major research hospital. As soon as a baby is born, the cord is removed, tested for any infectious agents and frozen for future use by the baby or transplanted into a compatible donor.

---

[174] Adam and Kim Lewis. *The Goodness of God.* Bethany Christian Services ,6 April 2006.
http://www.bethany.org/A55798/bethanyWWW.nsf/c79edbd86c517a1d852 569c800702556/f2d2700f1830a72d852571260066666b?OpenDocument

It is a strange day when Presidents are asked to enter the debate. On May 24th 2005, George Bush announced a landmark decision to fund stem cell research projects. He drew the line on funding new embryonic stem cell development. Here is part of his speech:

> "I believe America must pursue the tremendous possibilities of science, and I believe we can do so while still fostering and encouraging respect for human life in all its stages. In the complex debate over embryonic stem cell research, we must remember that real human lives are involved -- both the lives of those with diseases that might find cures from this research, and the lives of the embryos that will be destroyed in the process. The children here today are reminders that every human life is a precious gift of matchless value.[175]

The group he made the announcement to was the parents of adopted frozen embryos. There were twenty-one babies in the room at the time of his speech. All of them had been frozen embryos before they were adopted.

> "The children here today remind us that there is no such thing as a spare embryo. Every embryo is unique and genetically complete, like every other human being. And each of us started out our life this way. These lives are not raw material to be exploited, but gifts. And I commend each of the families here today for accepting the gift of these children and offering them the gift of your love."[176]

On the critical question as to why stem cell research and certain types of cloning techniques are unethical, James Sherley, an Associate Professor of Biological Engi-

---

[175] George W. Bush. *President Discusses Embryo Adoption and Ethical Stem Cell Research.* The White House News, 24 May 2005 14:07 EDT. http://www.whitehouse.gov/news/releases/2005/05/20050524-12.html
[176] Ibid.

neering at the Massachusetts Institute of Technology, gives his views:

> "Despite the confusion that some like to create on the questions of 'are embryos human beings?' and 'when does a human life begin?', both scientists and physicians know very well that human embryos are alive and human. A human life begins when a diploid complement of human DNA is initiated to begin human development. Therefore, a life can be initiated by the fusion of sperm and egg or by the introduction of a diploid nucleus into an enucleated egg (ie, 'cloning')."[177]

So far, the only real breakthroughs in stem cell therapy are through using adult stem cells and cord stem cells. Leukemia patients have benefited for over forty years by blood stem cells reproducing bone marrow. There have been no proven therapies developed using embryonic stem cells and many researchers believe it is still very far off. It is just too difficult to get these embryonic cells to act the way scientists want them to.

Thanks to the pro-life movement, the church has a head start in this particular area of biotechnology and bioethics. Back in the trenches of the abortion debate, we developed our theology of the unborn. But what about the technologies which alter the very inception of life? One could argue that to be against cloning makes us anti-life.

Hello Dolly

There is a picture you would find on many postcards from Scotland of one fully-grown ewe and three little lambs by her side. Dolly was born on July 5th 1996.[178] What makes

---

[177] Michael Cook. *To clone or not to clone.* Mercatornet. 6 December 2005. http://www.mercatornet.com/index.php?option=com_content&task=view&id=193/

[178] My sources for research on the topic *Dolly the Sheep* are:

Dolly different is that she came from only one genetic parent. Dolly is the first known mammal to be cloned from an adult DNA. There had been other animals cloned before Dolly using embryonic cells. Her cousins Megan and Morag were born a year earlier using this technique. Like her cousins, Dolly was conceived in the laboratories of the Roslin Institute in Edinburgh, Scotland. She was originally designated "6LL3." She was renamed Dolly in honor of Dolly Parton because a mammary stem cell from a six-year-old ewe was used to clone her. John Kilner, Senior Scholar at the Center for Bioethics and Human Dignity, gives one of the simplest explanations of how a clone is made.

"We have long known that virtually every cell of the body contains a person's complete genetic code. The exception is sperm or egg cells, which each contain half the genetic material until the sperm fertilizes the egg and a new human being with a complete genetic code begins growing. We have now learned that the partial genetic material in a female's unfertilized egg cell may be removed and replaced by the complete genetic material from a cell taken from an adult. With a full genetic code, the egg cell behaves as if it has been fertilized and begins to grow. At least, that's what happened in a sheep."[179]

- The Science Museum Antenna:
  http://www.sciencemuseum.org.uk/antenna/dolly/index.asp
- *Dolly the Sheep*. Wikipedia, the Free Encyclopedia. 6 April 2006 UTC:
  http://en.wikipedia.org/wiki/Dolly_the_sheep
- The Roslin Institute which was the responsible for cloning Dolly:
  http://www.roslin.ac.uk/public/cloning.html
- The Center for Bioethics and Human Dignity – Cloning:
  http://www.cbhd.org/resources/cloning/index.html
- Mercatornet Newsletter:
  http://www.mercatornet.com/index.php?option=com_content&task=view&id=193/

[179] John F. Kilner. *An Overview of Human Cloning*. The Center for Bioethics and Human Dignity. Copyright 2001 6 April 2006.
http://www.cbhd.org/resources/cloning/overview.htm

Dolly lived to give birth to three of her own genetically normal sheep. She was considered healthy and normal until, after four years, signs of arthritis began to show up in her joints. She died at age six on February 14th 2003, about half the age of a healthy sheep. It was announced that she had progressive lung disease; a disease that was not considered abnormal for sheep her age that had to live indoors as Dolly had most of her life. It was discovered that her arthritis was quite advanced and several types of cells in her body appeared older than normal. Could this be the six years of her genetic parent plus her six years? Scientists are unwilling to commit to this theory of her early death.

Since Dolly, the list of animals that have been cloned using this same method is growing. They include tadpole, carp, sheep, pig, gaur, cattle, cat, mice, rabbit, mule, deer, horse, rat, fruit flies, and dog.[180]

In 2004 a Korean scientist claimed he had cloned a human embryo but it was later proven that he falsified his research. In May of 2005, British Scientists successfully cloned four embryos, three of them survived for three days and one for five days.[181] The British have the most liberal laws on cloning in the world and have allowed the cloning of embryos for "therapeutic cloning." This is allowed in Britain to give researchers the chance to clone for treating disease and disability. "Reproductive cloning" is for the purpose of creating a baby and was made illegal in Britain in 2001. The obvious moral dilemma is that an embryo is in fact already a baby.

This is Greg and my other Clone Greg

Why does the world seem to be rushing down this slope toward cloning humans? Most scientists would an-

---

[180] *List of animals that have been cloned.* Wikipedia, The Free Encyclopedia. 6 April 2006 17:27 UTC
http://en.wikipedia.org/wiki/List_of_animals_that_have_been_cloned
[181] *UK scientists clone human embryo.* BBC News. 20 May 2005 11:53 UK
http://news.bbc.co.uk/1/hi/health/4563607.stm

swer "because we can." Certainly, this captures the spirit of science today, which does not seem to have many ethical moorings holding them down. Dr. William Cheshire writes for The Center for Bioethics and Human Dignity:

> "'The development of human cloning is inevitable,' testified the controversial fertility researcher Panayiotis Zavos before Congress. His words a year ago seem strangely prophetic now that Advanced Cell Technology has claimed that its laboratories have produced the first cloned human embryos.
>
> "What was once a fantasy flowing from the ink pens of science fiction writers is on the verge of oozing from the pipettes of a few impetuous biotech entrepreneurs. The means to replicate genetically identical young copies - clones - of a human person may be very nearly, and perhaps irresistibly, within the grasp of existing technology."[182]

The idea that something is inevitable is really a form of Technological Determinism. This way of thinking tells us that, "We have no choice. Our technological path will lead in this direction and there is nothing we can do."

There are other, possibly good reasons for cloning and many of these reasons are already being brought to life through our main cultural gathering place, the cinema. Here are some of the typical reasons given for cloning which are mirrored by the movies:

- By having clones, people can exert more influence upon the world. This was portrayed in the 1978 movie, *The Boys from Brazil,* staring Gregory Peck, where a group of Nazis attempted to clone Adolph Hitler.
- Parents can replace a dying child with a genetically identical new one. The 2004 movie, *Godsend*, staring

---

[182] William P. Cheshire Jr. *Human Cloning and the Ethics of Inevitability.* The Center for Bioethics and Human Dignity. 25 January 2005 http://www.cbhd.org/resources/cloning/cheshire_2002-01-25.htm

Robert De Niro, is about cloning a couple's deceased son. The clone, though genetically a match, turned out very different from their son.

- Clones can be produced to provide spare parts for their genetic parent. These clones would be for therapeutic purposes. In the 2005 movie, *The Island*, starring Ewan McGregor and Scarlett Johansson, clones are manufactured and wait until their parts are needed. They are given a simple but pampered life. The clones gain a sense of who they are and escape.

- Clones could work for us and enable us to be in more than one place at a time. In the 1996 movie, *Multiplicity,* starring Michael Keaton, clones enable a man with a busy life to be in two places at once.

- We could retrain clones to live and work the way we want them to. Clones could be used to do things and act in ways that their genetic parent would not. In the 2004 movie, *The Stepford Wives*, starring Nicole Kidman and Matthew Broderick, disgruntled husbands clone their wives and kill the originals. The clones are trained to act in a submissive manner.

- Clones could be used for the menial, unpleasant and dangerous tasks that we have to partake in, such as simple labor, dirty jobs and fighting wars. In the 2002 movie, *Star Wars – the Attack of the Clones*, a cloned army is used in warfare.

If Zavos is right, "the development of human cloning is inevitable," then this generation will need to answer some of the most difficult questions ever faced by mankind. Are human clones really human? Do they have a spirit and are they in the image of God? What should we do with a clone? Should we discriminate based on cloning? Can a clone be saved?

Belle – the Telekinetic Monkey

Scientists at Duke University[183] developed a small cap with little wire electrodes coming out of the inside. It resembles a brush with tiny hairs coming out of the cap's center. Belle is a very intelligent owl monkey that had learned to play a game with a joystick, two lights and a fruit juice dispenser. When the left light turned on, she would move the joystick to the left with her tiny little hand and be rewarded with a squirt of fruit juice. When Belle had mastered the game, the research team cut away a piece of her skull and planted about 100 of the electrodes inside her brain. These were attached to her motor cortex. Using the digital signals coming from Belle's brain, the research team was able to wire her to a robotic arm via a computer in the next room. In time, they trained Belle to communicate with the robot arm telekinetically and achieved the same results as she had with her natural arm. Essentially, Belle became a telekinetic monkey who controlled robots with her mind.

The story of Belle may or may not seem that earth-shattering to you. But consider that scientist have directly wired probes into a mammal's brain and networked a computer to it. Did you get that? They networked a computer to a brain! The next step was much easier than connecting to the brain; the team connected a similar arm at M.I.T., 600 miles north of Duke University. This duplicate arm mimicked the motion of the arm that Belle was manipulating. This meant that a monkey was moving a robot 600 miles away with her brain over the internet. A monkey, the internet, robots – did you get that?

---

[183] I researched the following sources on Belle the Telekinetic Monkey:
- o Elton Cronin. *Potential in the Brain.* Project Magazine, Fall 2003 http://promag.cfes.ca/article.php?article=20-03-04
- o Miguel A. L. Nicolelis and John K. Chapin. *Controlling Robots with the Mind.* Scientific American, 16 September 2002 http://touchlab.mit.edu/news/documents/ScinetificAmerican_2002.pdf
- o Joel Garreau. *Radical Evolution: The Promise and Peril of Enhancing Our Minds, Our Bodies -- and What It Means to Be Human.* Double-day, May 2005. Pages 19-20

This remarkable technology, called Brain-Machine Interfaces (BMI), will be a tremendous blessing to those who are handicapped. It won't be long before a quadriplegic will be able to command their wheel chair or prosthetic limbs using BMI technology. In an interview with Scientific American, the researchers from Duke commented on their progress:

"In the two years since that day, our labs and several others have advanced neuroscience, computer science, microelectronics and robotics to create ways for rats, monkeys and eventually humans to control mechanical and electronic machines purely by 'thinking through,' or imagining, the motions. Our immediate goal is to help a person who has been paralyzed by a neurological disorder or spinal cord injury, but whose motor cortex is spared, to operate a wheelchair or a robotic limb. Someday the research could also help such a patient regain control over a natural arm or leg, with the aid of wireless communication between implants in the brain and the limb. And it could lead to devices that restore or augment other motor, sensory or cognitive functions."[184]

This is already happening with the new hearing aids for the profoundly deaf. Cochlear implants have been around since 1973 and connect directly to the brain. A microphone is implanted in the ear which sends sound to a speech processor. The processor converts the sound to an electronic signal that is sent to the brain and understood.[185] It is wired to the hearing center of the brain. The miracle of this process is that we really don't know exactly where to wire to; the brain takes over and adapts to the stimuli sent by the electrodes.

---

[184] Miguel A. L. Nicolelis and John K. Chapin. *Controlling Robots with the Mind.* Scientific American, 16 September 2002
http://touchlab.mit.edu/news/documents/ScinetificAmerican_2002.pdf
[185] *Cochlear Implants.* NIH Publication No. 00-4798, November 2002
http://www.nidcd.nih.gov/health/hearing/coch.asp

It is only a matter of time before we wire ourselves to computers. In this age of wireless technology, we could have a little, wireless network device connected to a cranial implant. With your thoughts, you could be browsing Google inside of your head. Tap the initiate button on the side of your skull and on flashes something similar to a computer screen; focus on any flat surface and the web page appears. Hyperlink to what you want to know and, voila, it is there before you. If you want to meditate on the Word, point your brain to www.BibleGateway.com and their new cerebral-voice-reader gently and quietly reads the book of John in your head. In a new wireless world, high-speed internet will be as available as cell phone networks. Tap your head again and, snap, it is turned off. No more Ipods, cell phones, radios and pocket PCs, just digitally wired brains; thanks to a little monkey named Belle.

More Human or More Machine

Those of us who are *Star Trek* fans will never forget the scariest moment in the series' history. I have watched every episode of the early *Star Trek* and *Next Generation*, almost every episode of *Deep Space Nine* and *Voyager* and about seventy-five percent of the most recent series called *Enterprise*. I have also seen all ten *Star Trek* movies. I enjoyed the shows because of the cool special effects, but mostly because they deal with present-day issues in a futuristic context. Many of the issues discussed in this book are the subject of episodes that deal with the various ethics and difficulties new technology will cause. Oh yeah, and I plan to travel to Vulcan one day in the future.

The most frightening moment of any episode or movie I recall is when our beloved Captain Picard was assimilated and became Locutus of Borg. Borg are an alien species that combine themselves with technology. They assimilate any race of people and accumulate their intelligence. This adds to their collective growth toward perfection. They add the assimilated species to their collective mind. They are linked, or networked, through implants that allow them to think and act as one mind. All individuality is lost in the billions of Borg that make up the singular consciousness.

There stood Picard, completely controlled and given over to the Borg. His frightening figure as a machine merged with flesh appeared on the video screen before the crew of the *Starship Enterprise*. He announced to all humanity, "We are the Borg. We will add your biological and technological distinctiveness to our own. Resistance is futile. You will be assimilated." He was then used by the Borg to nearly destroy the entire Federation Space Fleet. Thankfully, Commander Riker, along with a creative screenplay, captured Picard and saved what was left of the fleet.

This doomsday scenario is so scary because it is so plausible in our world today. We are melding ourselves with technology in ways that could absorb our very humanity. Today it is possible to become a cyborg[186] or someone who becomes part human and part machine. We are again faced with the question, "what makes us human." John Kilner and Ben Mitchell from The Center for Bioethics and Human Dignity begin to answer this question.

"Robots and computers will of course never become human. Why not? Because being 'one of us' transcends functional biology. Human beings are psychosomatic soulish unities made in the image of God. The image of God is fully located neither in our brain nor our DNA. We, and all who are 'one of us,' are unique combinations of body, soul, and mind. We might quibble theologically about how best to describe the components of our humanity, but most Christians agree that we are more than the sum of our biological and functional parts."[187]

---

[186] *Cyborg.* Wikipedia, The Free Encyclopedia. 7 April 2006 09:41 UTC http://en.wikipedia.org/wiki/Cyborg

[187] C. Ben Mitchell and John F. Kilner. *Remaking Humans: The New Utopians Versus a Truly Human Future.* The Center for Bioethics and Human Dignity, 29 August 2003

We are spirit, soul and body[188] not just a body as Naturalism, Darwinism and secular humanism teaches. Our bodies are the part of us that contacts this physical realm and our spirits are the part of us that contacts the spiritual realm. Unlike animals we are able to transcend the physical. And unlike angels we are able to freely live in the physical realm. We are, indeed, created in the image of God.[189] As Kliner and Mitchell pointed out "being 'one of us' transcends functional biology." Ultimately we are not just physical, biological beings. We have a responsibility as stewards of our bodies to ensure that we do not violate the sacred boundaries God has placed on how far we should go.

Do you not know that your body is a temple of the Holy Spirit, who is in you, whom you have received from God? You are not your own; you were bought at a price. Therefore honor God with your body.
1 Corinthians 6:19-20 (NIV)

Technology has a habit of sneaking up on us and captivating our lives before we realize what is happening to us. These transcendent technologies can be very deceptive; are we able to discern their potential before we accept and commit to use them?

This new world of genetic engineering, stem cell manipulation, cloning and the melding of flesh to machine will create the biggest questions in history about our humanity and what it means to be human. Are you ready to answer these questions? Are you preparing yourself for the deci-

---

http://www.cbhd.org/resources/bioethics/mitchell_kilner_2003-08-29_print.htm

[188] 1 Thessalonians 5:23 (NIV) *May God himself, the God of peace, sanctify you through and through. May your whole spirit, soul and body be kept blameless at the coming of our Lord Jesus Christ.*

[189] Genesis 1:26 (NIV) *Then God said, "Let us make man in our image, in our likeness, and let them rule over the fish of the sea and the birds of the air, over the livestock, over all the earth, and over all the creatures that move along the ground."*

sions our culture will press upon us? What technology will you approve of, and what technology will you deem too dangerous. How far will you go with the merger of machines in your experience?

Our children and grandchildren must begin to face these human defining questions in our culture. Here is just a taste of what they must answer:

- What type of genetic alteration is acceptable to God?
- What safeguards do we need to place on science and scientists?
- What forms of discrimination will we tolerate between enhanced humans and natural humans?
- What types of enhancements are unacceptable?
- Should we try to find answers to every disease?
- Is it moral to destroy embryos in order to save another's life?
- What do we do with the millions of embryos being created?
- Can we alter human life in the embryonic stages to produce body parts for those who are in need?
- Should we attempt to clone human beings?
- Is a cloned human being in the image of God? Does she or it have a spirit?
- What will be the ethical issues involved with clones?
- Should we discriminate against clones?
- How should we use clones in our culture?
- Can a clone accept Jesus as their Savior and receive eternal life?
- What kinds of inclusion of machines are acceptable?
- Should we wire our brains to computers?
- How many cybernetic implants are too many?
- Will we loose our humanity in the machines?

Jesus is the only true fountain of life. No matter how we answer these questions, He will be mankind's only answer for true fulfillment. Jesus is the true superman and we get to be like him.

Section Three

The Digital Future

"Technological Progress is like an axe in the hands of a pathological criminal."

Albert Einstein,
Letter to a friend, 1917

The Doubling

"...Most important principal - exponential thinking."[190]

Rick Warren
Author of the *Purpose Driven Life*

In a land far away there lived a wealthy king. He was strict with his subjects and exacted very high taxes, but he was honest in his judgment and his word was always true. His son became ill and all of the kingdom's physicians were unable to find a cure. Word was sent throughout the kingdom that if anyone found a cure the king would reward that subject handsomely, up to one quarter of his kingdom.

One of the peasants who worked in the castle helping the chief steward with the castle bookkeeping noticed that the food being prepared for the son contained walnuts and he himself had often become ill while eating these nuts. He told the chef to stop using the nuts and in two days, the boy was well. When the king found out who had brought forth the wise council, he called the peasant bean counter to his chambers.

---

[190] This statement is made in the first minutes of: *Exponential Thinking*. 40 Days of Purpose Overview Video. Purpose Driven, 2004. Rick said this at a Pastor's conference where he was trying to convince church leaders to think in much bigger numbers than they were used to.

The king was beside himself when he announced, "You have saved my son and, more importantly, the heir to my wealth and kingdom." The king continued, "Up to one quarter of my kingdom is at your disposal; what shall I grant you?"

The peasant replied in a very humble manner, "Great king, you are fair and your word is always sure. I will only ask for a humble portion." He knew exactly how to stroke the king's ego, "I ask for a simple thing: that I might feed my son and provide for his needs. Would you, oh great king, please observe that I have brought a chess board to your chambers."

The peasant pointed to the corner and sure enough, there was the board. He brought it before the king and continued, "I humbly ask that you would place one bean on the next square of the board each day and have it delivered to my home and storehouse." He paused for effect as he placed a bean on the corner square.

"Is that all you ask?" inquired the king with a puzzled look.

"One more detail, your majesty," replied the peasant. "You are a great and mighty king; would you also double the beans each day so that I receive twice the amount from the day before? I beg the king and his court's indulgence on this matter." The peasant looked timidly around the chambers and continued. "Today I am given one bean and tomorrow, two, the next day, four and the next day, eight, until the entire board is full."

The king looked at his chief assistant who was shaking his head with a bewildered look. He advised, "I think this will more than adequately requite the gentleman, sire."

The king turned and pronounced, "Let it be so. As I give my oath and kingdom, so you shall be rewarded with the beans." He paused the way kings do in such officious pronouncements, "Ah, we shall call it: The Doubling."

Papers were prepared and documents signed. The king's word was law.

Each day the chief was ordered to come and add the beans. A royal courier was assigned to deliver the beans.

Each day brought new banter in the chambers. Even on day ten when the tired chief brought out the 512 beans for delivery, the court broke out in laughter. Some shouted, "Perhaps the peasant can make his son bean soup today!"

Nobody had any idea what to expect in the coming weeks. On day fourteen, they had their first crisis. The chief could not find enough beans in the palace storehouse to provide the 8,192 beans. For the first time, two weeks into the agreement, the chief wondered what he would do tomorrow.

Over the next few days, the king's steward solved the problem by taxing the kingdom's subjects beans instead of money. Everyone happily handed over their supply. By the third week the crisis returned. On this day, the king's servants delivered 1,048,576 beans. The king himself was desperately worried about keeping his word. He sent ships and armies out to find every bean within two weeks' distance of the kingdom. He began to glimpse his fate.

All was lost on day thirty when the king could not provide the 536,870,912 beans. Realizing that he still had thirty-four squares of the chessboard remaining, he summoned the peasant.

With as much dignity that he could muster, the king said, "I have failed in my oath. I have forsworn my kingdom. I am in your hands"

"Indeed you are," retorted the former peasant. "I will have your entire kingdom. I will have all of your goods and I will have your crown."

The honest king had no choice. He relinquished his crown, stepped aside and left the kingdom. Rumor has it that he started a bean farm.

Exponential "Doubling" or Back to Moore's Law

In 2002 the twenty-seventh doubling of the computer chip occurred.[191] The billion-transistor DRAM chip came rolling off the Intel assembly line.

---

[191] George Gilder. *Moore's Quantum Leap*. Wired Magazine, Jan. 2002. http://www.wired.com/wired/archive/10.01/gilder.html "Why has the mi-

Remember Moore's Law - Gordon E. Moore, co-founder of the technology giant, Intel? More than half of all computer chips in the world come from his company. "Moore's law" is based on the amount of transistors that can be put on a computer chip at relatively the same size and cost. Every two years, or more precisely, every eighteen months, computer power has continued to double since 1962. This is known as an exponential curve.

This means that computer chips will be able to hold eight-billion transistors by 2008. When will it slow down?

The curve began back in 1826, when Joseph Henry sent digital signals to his schoolboys in the next room. The first double was in about 1840, when Henry Morris created his code and stole a few patents. In 1868, the transcontinental telegraph cable was laid; double number three, and on through the next century with an invention here and an innovation there; double, double, double, double. In the 1920s and 30s we see doubling in the inventions of radio and television; double. In the 40s, the first digital computers were used; double. Alan Turning's theories of digital computing resulted in scientists all over the world considering ways that they too could create computers. Pick it up again in the 1950s, when the properties of silicon were discovered—double. Here the exponential curve began to really take off and double quicker. IBM began to build the first true "Supercomputer" called the 7000 series mainframe—double. IBM began using disks to store data—double. The first true transistor-based computers were made public in 1960—double. In 1964, a much smaller machine is launched for mid-sized laboratories—double. In the mid-sixties, the microprocessor hit the scene—double. Throughout the seventies, we saw the innovation of microcomputers being invented and programmed by guys in their garage—double. Tandy comes out with a desktop computer that has a processor working at 16 kilobytes a second—double. The 8086 processor was invented in the early eighties and more

crochip's explosive growth rate never happened before? George Gilder explains the micro microeconomics and why silicon is just the beginning."

IBM computers became available for about $10,000 a machine—double. Apple launched the Macintosh desktop PC with their famous super-bowl ad—double. In 1986 the Intel introduced the 286 microprocessor chip—double. In 1988 the 386; double. In 1991, the 486—double. Then we saw the Pentiums I, II, III—double—double—double . At the turn of the millennium, the Pentium IVs—double. Since we started using the IV, they have doubled three times. As soon as you buy a computer, no matter how powerful it is, its shelf life for resale is about four months—double. As you can plainly see everything is doubling much quicker. The exponential curve is climbing very quickly right now.[192]

Thankfully, what is not doubling is all of the support technology necessary for the transistor-laden chip. Motherboards and other hardware components are still catching up to the processor chip. Contrary to what Microsoft and Adobe want you to believe, software is not doubling every two years. Software is the way we take advantage of the computer and make it do what we want. Software is also on an exponential curve but is only doubling about every five years at this point.

Other technologies and innovations have gone through doubling growth spurts but not so consistently and for such a prolonged period. The railroads doubled through the mid-nineteenth century but began to slow when there were no more places to go. Joel Garreau writes about this in his chapter entitled *The Curve*.

"This astonishing power has become almost free because, unlike the railroads, its expansion does not have the material limits of, say, Grand Central Station. The cost of shipping a ton of grain was halved perhaps three times during the railroads' heyday. The cost of computing had halved almost 30 times by the early 21st Century. There are only four limits to computer evolution: quantum physics, human ingenuity,

---

[192] *History of computing hardware.* Wikipedia, The Free Encyclopedia. 7 April 2006 21:53 UTC
http://en.wikipedia.org/wiki/History_of_computing_hardware

the market and our will. Actually, it's not at all clear that there are any practical limits represented by quantum physics, human ingenuity and the market, at least not in our lifetimes."[193]

Don't forget our little tale at the beginning of this chapter. On day 30, the king had to surrender his throne. Today is day 29 in computing. Doubling the processor power of today's computer means a heck-of-a-lot more than the doubling of the IBM monster computer called Deep Blue. This is the computer that beat world chess champion, Gary Kasparov, in 1997. It was upgraded after its 1996 loss against Kasparov. Capable of evaluating 200,000,000 positions per second, it was now twice as fast as the 1996 version.[194] Compare this with today's monster supercomputer, Blue Gene. It has 1000 times more processing power than its ancestor, Deep Blue. In order to describe how fast and how much it can do, we are making up words such as "teraFLOPS" and "petaFLOPS."[195] I won't even try to define these terms. Let's just say they are really, really big numbers. Okay, I cannot resist: FLOPS are known as Floating point Operations Per Second. A gigaFLOP is a billion FLOPS. Pentium 4 computers can perform at several GFLOPS. TeraFLOPS are a trillion flops and petaFLOPS are a thousand trillion (quadrillion) FLOPS. The first petaFLOPS-capable computer will be rolling out sometime by the end of this year. As I said before, really, really big numbers.

---

[193] Joel Garreau. *Radical Evolution: The Promise and Peril of Enhancing Our Minds, Our Bodies -- and What It Means to Be Human.* Doubleday, May 2005; The Curve, Page 52

[194] *Deep Blue.* Wikipedia, The Free Encyclopedia. 27 March 2006 01:24 UTC http://en.wikipedia.org/wiki/Deep_Blue

[195] *Flops.* Wikipedia, The Free Encyclopedia. 5 April 2006 20:02 UTC http://en.wikipedia.org/wiki/FLOPS

Nanotechnology – Smaller is Bigger

One of the main reasons why computers can continue to double is that for computers to advance, they must grow smaller instead of bigger. Remember that one of the measures for doubling is how many transistors can be placed on a microprocessor chip. Obviously, the smaller we can make these transistors, the more we can get on a chip.

Nanotechnology is a term for creating technology at the very smallest of sizes. A nanometer is one billionth of a meter. By comparison, the average sheet of paper is 100,000 nanometers thick. Here is how the National Nanotechnology Initiative website defines it:

"Nanotechnology is the understanding and control of matter at dimensions of roughly 1 to 100 nanometers, where unique phenomena enable novel applications. Encompassing nanoscale science, engineering and technology, nanotechnology involves imaging, measuring, modeling, and manipulating matter at this length scale.

"At the nanoscale, the physical, chemical, and biological properties of materials differ in fundamental and valuable ways from the properties of individual atoms and molecules or bulk matter. Nanotechnology R&D is directed toward understanding and creating improved materials, devices, and systems that exploit these new properties."[196]

Nanotechnology is finding its way into commercial products. If you use certain sunscreen or cosmetics, water filtration, sunglasses or even tennis rackets, then it is possible your product has been developed with nanotechnology. Wal-Mart will soon be using nano-identifiers to track their products. Sprinkle on a little nano-dust, pass it under a scanner and they can track what you buy.

---

[196] *What is Nanotechnology?* National Nanotechnology Initiative Website, April 9, 2006. http://www.nano.gov/html/facts/whatIsNano.html

Nanotechnology research is huge in the medical industry and pharmaceuticals. This new field is called Biomolecular Nanotechnology, or in other words, working at the molecular level of biology. Scientists are experimenting with miniature robots that can attach themselves to a cell in the body and administer medicine or surgically alter the cell. Beyond this, they will be able to manipulate a DNA molecule by sending a specific nano-agent that will find a particular gene and remove or alter it.

In a paper published for the annual review of Biomedical Engineering, the scientists at the research center for Bio-Nano Robotics at Northeastern University explain the breakthrough work they are doing.

Mother Nature has her own set of molecular machines that have been working for centuries and have become optimized for performance and design over the ages. As our knowledge and understanding of these numerous machines continues to increase, we now see a possibility of using the natural machines, or creating synthetic ones from scratch, by mimicking nature... The ever-increasing computing power makes it possible to dynamically model protein folding processes and predict the conformations and structure of lesser known proteins. These findings help unravel the mysteries associated with the molecular machinery and pave the way for the production and application of these miniature machines in various fields, including medicine, space exploration, electronics and military.[197]

"The ever-increasing computing power makes it possible..."—double.

---

[197] Mavroidis, C., Dubey, A., and Yarmush, M. *Molecular Machines.* Annual Review of Biomedical Engineering, 2004. Vol. 6, Page. 364
http://www.coe.neu.edu/Research/robots/papers/annurev.pdf

Computer Doubling will Double Almost Everything

Gordon Moore has since revised his predictions and indicates that computer technology doubling will start to slow down by 2016 when the microchip circuitry is working at 1 to 100 nanometers.[198] Essentially this is as small as the most minute molecule. It means we will build computers out of circuitry two and half times smaller than the DNA Molecule.[199] Intel recently announced they have produced transistors of which its smallest features are 90 nanometers wide.

Joel Garreau shows how the computer's doubling is affecting other areas outside of the microchip:

"Meanwhile, the amount of computer memory you can get for a dollar is doubling every 15 months. The cost-performance ratio of Internet service providers is doubling every 12 months... Internet backbone band-width is doubling every 12 months. The size of the Internet is doubling every 12 months. In short, the number of other curves of accelerated change unleashed by Moore's Law have themselves begun to proliferate exponentially.

"Human genes mapped per year—doubling time, 18 months. Resolution of brain-scanning devices—doubling time, 12 months. Growth in personal and service robots—doubling time, 9 months."[200]

---

[198] Gordon E. Moore. *No Exponential is Forever...* Intel, 2003. ftp://download.intel.com/research/silicon/Gordon_Moore_ISSCC_021003.pdf

[199] The National Nanotechnology Initiative has an excellent scale depicting the various sizes of very small things, from an ant, 5mm, to atoms of silicon .1 nm. A picture is worth a teraflop of words. http://www.nano.gov/html/facts/The_scale_of_things.html

[200] Joel Garreau. *Radical Evolution: The Promise and Peril of Enhancing Our Minds, Our Bodies -- and What It Means to Be Human.* Doubleday, May 2005 The Curve, page 58-59

The Barna Group has reported doublings in the use of technology and the internet among Christians.[201]

Where will this all lead to? How much doubling can we sustain until something extremely dramatic happens - if it hasn't already! The French are trying to help their children understand what is happening.

"French children are told a story in which you imagine having a pond with water lily leaves floating on the surface. The lily doubles in size every day and if left unchecked will smother the pond in 30 days, killing all the other living things in the water. Day after day the plant seems small and so you decide to leave it grow until it half-covers the pond, before cutting it back. On what day will that occur? The 29th day, and then you will have just one day to save the pond."[202]

It is day 29 in computing doubling. Something is going to happen soon. According to our French tale, today is the last day to do something about it.

The Digital World in 2016

Change has come upon us so fast that to try and predict what will happen in the next ten years is like trying to see through my set of really bad binoculars. I can see things at a distance but I see two of everything. If I try to align the two lenses, it all goes funny. Nearly every prediction we can make has two possible ways it can go. Things can get better or things can get worse depending upon how

---

[201] *Americans Embrace Technologies that Bring Control to their Lives.* The Barna Research Group, Ltd., Ventura, CA, April 1, 2003.
http://www.barna.org/FlexPage.aspx?Page=BarnaUpdate&BarnaUpdateID=136
[202] *Exponential Increase.* Wikipedia, The Free Encyclopedia. *Exponential stories; The water lily.* 29 March 2006 17:42 UTC
http://en.wikipedia.org/wiki/Exponential_increase

you focus your viewpoint. The following are some of my predictions. I will categorize them based on the Four Digital Transformations. My predictions and scenarios are based upon relative world stability and that the present pace of digital progress is allowed to continue.

Let me preface my predictions with two disclaimers. First, I am not an expert on any of the areas I am going to postulate. I am a pastor and an educator. If I have any expertise it is in the area of discipleship. I would not recommend that you base your personal stock portfolio on my predictions. Secondly, I am not functioning under any prophetic mantle that I know of. I am not relying on some special revelation of the Holy Spirit. I am using my plane old noggin. If I get anything right then the glory goes to God who supplied me with the information and wisdom in the first place. For what I get wrong, you can say, 'I knew that guy was whacked!'

Communication in 2016:

Communication technological convergence has brought all of the mediums to the internet. We can now watch every movie (when it is released to the net from the theaters), television show and video-cast wherever we want, whenever we want. Every bit of media can now be found and accessed on the net including any book, music set (formally CD), radio broadcast, podcast, etc. They are all simply accessed by your Personal Net-Device.

My Personal Net-Device (PND) is now my notebook computer, cell phone, PDA, Ipod, global positioning device, web browser, etc. It is always connected to the internet since the cellular phone networks were adapted a few years ago. I am constantly wired to the internet just about anywhere in the world. I just set the device down near any video monitor which I then use for large scale computing. I can type on any flat surface near the unit but I prefer to talk with it; that way I can work faster and sometimes it comes up with really cool ideas.

When I come home, my door opens for me as my DNA signature is scanned. Each room I walk into, the lights adjust automatically. I ask Mabel, my HCI (Home Computer Interface – installed right next to the electrical panel; Mabel is what we call our house now) what is available on video. It sifts through my list of preferences and sees that the latest Peter Jackson film has just been released to the net. I can hardly wait to watch it on my newly installed wall video. I will have to kick my wife off. She is shopping for groceries on it. She prefers this over the old monitor connection because she can read the labels better. I have suggested to her that she relies on Mabel to use the QMRS (Quantity Measurement Replacement System) in the kitchen but she prefers to be old-fashioned and do the shopping herself. I make a mental note to ask Mabel to see about upgrading the content filter. There is no telling what wickedness can come through these big screens. The wall unit will also be nice for my v-classroom work. I should be able to see every student's work up close. This will be especially helpful in the music and art classes.

Mabel has just indicated that my missionary brother in Haiti has sent me an e-message. I instruct her to give it to me in the bedroom. As I am changing, his voice comes bounding into the room. For a moment, I have to stop and think, *is he looking at me?* He asks me to v-message. As I button up my shirt, I tell Mabel to put it on the TV in the room. The message is very sketchy as Haiti is still on the old hard-wired internet system. After a few moments, Mabel makes the necessary adjustments. My brother introduces me to his newest convert. Fortunately, I have just upgraded my translation interface. We talk for almost an hour. I update my v-log (video blog) by editing some of this interview with my new Haitian friend. I ask Mabel to reference it and send it to all of my brother's supporters.

When someone is involved in suspicious activity over the net, their communication access is suspended or curtailed. A good hacker can get around this but in two or three years every PND, HCI and any other access device will be upgraded to DNA recognition. Unless the hackers can somehow alter their DNA, they won't be allowed access. Hackers are working on this as well.

The biggest crisis in communications is finding a specialist to maintain the hardware infrastructure. Thankfully, it is not hard to consult with the experts in India. They are usually quite good when you are able to isolate the problem. They magically fix the problem from their palatial homes in Bangalore.

The Counter-Cyber-Terrorism Group will be the next big Department of Defense program. Already they have shut down dozens of fundamentalist communication rings. They have successfully turned away virus attacks on the National Cloning Facilities. They are about to expose the Anti-Embryo-Destruction League through decoding their internet ciphers. I hope they don't link anything to me.

Globalization in 2016:

There are still parts of the world not on the wireless network. Google is making sure that in the next year or two there will not be any more "wireless divide." Most people are able to use technology because it is so easy and intuitive. Gone are the days of having to type commands, even in the third world.

Our church and school are still trying to get around the access restrictions to China. You would think such a technological culture would be more aware. I have v-messaged several of the young Christian leaders but this is risky. One of them was almost caught - which would mean certain imprisonment. Chinese officials are finally beginning to wise up to the age-old prejudices against Christians. They are able to construe these communications as signs of pro-life activity not just of anti-Chinese political policies. Almost any Christian conversation is now somehow linked to the terrorist activities of the fundamentalist Anti-Embryo-Destruction League around the world.

The U.S. is still tightening its boarders but is now using the DNA registry to help identify those who are true citizens. There are still widespread protests to the registry but the technology is not invasive nor does it cause any harm, so it appears that the opposition will fade quickly.

The European Union announced they will begin negotiating a long-term agreement with Google and Intel. What makes this agreement so unusual is that it will be written with the language of national treaties. It will identify internet boundaries and populations and encourage the people of Europe to continue their allegiance to these companies. It will outline a new form of law enforcement. Under this agreement, terrorists will be arrested and tried through the new Google system of jurisprudence. Intel was invited into this agreement as a middle-of-the-road advocate for corporate politicization.

For the first time in over 100 years, the majority of the world's billionaires do not live in North America. The fastest growing sectors of wealth are in India followed by China, then Ireland.

Entrepreneur of the Year was given to a young, Indian engineer for his inter-language software translator. It will now work with any PND in the world.

The U.S. and NASA have finally agreed to give jurisdiction of the Mars project to the newly established United Nations Aeronautic Space Agency (UNASA). The President, in a resigned voice, said, "It took the cold war and the space race to get us to the moon. It will take a global economy and the internet to get us to Mars."

The World Congress for Cloning Technologies was held this year. It has not yet been decided if the multinationals will keep working with the prospective governments in developing policies for clone identification and use. The two most prominent voices in the congress were the British delegation, who demanded they have a say in how clones are perceived, and AjBiotech, the newly formed multinational company that owns 25 percent of the patents in the industry. They simply stated that Britain does not have the clout to make such demands.

Currency markets continue to slide as the new, so-called net-unit currency begins to stabilize. Paypal announced it has plans to buy out both VISA and MasterCard in one smooth transaction.

World-net features a young, African girl's v-log just before she is captured by Muslim extremists. She had been living in a Christian village in Uganda. She appeals to those of likeminded faith to do something about the terrible conditions and fear that her people are living under. Commentators debate over how important it is to stop things like this. One is quoted saying, "Religious thinking like this is a way of the past. It is unfortunate what happened to this girl but it is probably better in the long term. Let these religious intolerants kill each other."

Informationalism in 2016

Google announces they are now ready to begin indexing the National Genetic DNA Registry. Approximately 15 percent of the world has had their DNA sequenced but this announcement should cause the number to rise dramatically over the next few years. This list will enable scientists to study each and every genetic distinction. For less than $100 (80 net-units), anyone can register their own DNA. Just google your name, click the link marked "Genetic Info" and your doctor has instant access.

Intel announces that they have finally reached the ceiling of Moore's Law. They cannot get any smaller in their nanotechnology. This will have a specific impact upon the Google's genetic initiative. Sergey Brin appeared on World-net to announce that Google is investing five hundred billion dollars in research and development to explore other ways of computing. He said, "In order to process the entire biological genome of every living thing we need a little more oomph in our computers."

The Associated Global Christian Schools (AGCS) are the first to redefine their educational approach. They have collaborated with Microsoft, Google and NetEducator to design a critical thinking scope and sequence for Kindergarten to Grade 12. This new advance will still teach the basic skills of reading, writing and numeracy but from the start, will adopt an approach to critical thinking skills. Kids will still study the classics but everything will be designed to teach them how to think and how to search. Facts will take a back seat to thoughts and opinions.

A new field of psychology is opening up to deal with Information Overload Syndrome (IOS). This disease baffles physicians and psychiatrists. Increases in depression, insomnia and even some cases of amnesia have been traced to Information Overload. This branch of psychology will also deal with the opposite syndrome known as Internet Separation Anxiety Disorder (ISAD). This disease occurs when, for technical or social reasons, a person is cut off from the net. They go through severe depression and in some cases become catatonic. There are no known remedies to either syndrome at this time.

The first "foolproof" digital lock for protecting media content was delivered to the net. Artists, musicians and moviemakers were ecstatic! However, within hours, a hack was uploaded and free music and videos dominated the web traffic for over a week.

The newest supercomputer is said to think faster than the human brain. It can also access the entire database of human knowledge. Researchers have gathered from all over the world to seek wisdom from this machine. Its speech interface is so human and its answers so insightful, that many believe the machine has become sensifacient.[203] Working together, the computer and a group of scientists hammered out a document protecting the rights of the machine. When asked what religion the machine would choose after it had indexed all of the sacred books as well as thousands of years of religious history, gathering data from every recorded debate, it calmly replied that it had already become a Christian.

Biotechnology in 2016:

---

[203] "Converting into sensation." Webster's Revised Unabridged Dictionary. MICRA, Inc. © 1996, 1998

Eve, the first human clone, is turning 10 this year. She is normal in every physical and biological respect. She does seem a bit odd in her behavior but perhaps that can be attributed to growing up in a sequestered, adult environment. She has been prodded and poked, observed and studied, analyzed and calculated unlike any other ten-year-old. Even so, she still seems a bit too compliant.

The first wireless brain interface is ready for experimentation. This device wires an internet interface directly to the visual, hearing and motor centers of the human brain. Theoretically, a person will be able to surf and interact with the net directly from her brain. If all goes well with the testing over the next three years, it will be released for commercial distribution. By 2020 we could become one with the internet.

Legislation was passed through the World Corporate Conglomeration for Human Rights (WCCHR) to allow genetic enhancements worldwide. Up until now, no Global organization has taken this step. The organization approved the change fearing that some of the non-member regions, such as China and Korea, had already developed intellectually enhanced children. Such a head start could throw a huge imbalance of intellectual development in favor of those countries. One spokesperson commented, "We may already be too late."

The fifth annual conference for The Christian Global Response to Biotechnology met in Moscow. They are still divided over the issues that the WCCHR submitted to them for discernment. The argument over the ethics of human genetic enhancement almost turned into a brawl as some argued that God has given us this wisdom for altering our experience. Others argued that we are playing with the basics of life. Unable to reach a consensus, they submitted two statements of opposing positions. Needless to say, the WCCHR decided not to consult this group anymore.

The Bill and Melinda Gates Foundation announced that they have completely abolished malaria. This disease had at one time been the number one killer on the planet. The disease was eradicated through the combined efforts of the hundreds of organizations funded by the Foundation. Their resources are now focused on fighting the return of small pox. Like malaria, it was thought this disease was banished from the earth; only small strains were left tucked away in bio-labs. Due to an accident five years ago, the disease was re-released. Because mankind has no immunity to it, the virus spreads and kills all who are exposed to it. To date it has spread throughout western Africa and some parts of Spain and Portugal.

Another near disaster was averted this year. An MIT genetic experiment of a nano-bot designed to kill fungus in sewage systems got away from researchers during a lab accident. The bot showed up a few days later in the Boston municipal water supply. As it ate any available bacteria in the water system, it replicated itself at astonishing rates reaching exponential proportions. Fortunately, the city was able to isolate the infected area and stop circulation. The nano-bots started feeding on themselves and within days, the water system was reactivated. When the Food and Drug Administration investigated the incident, they found the scientists besides themselves with mortal fear. They realized that if the nano-bot fungus-eating machines had made it to the Atlantic Ocean, they would have, theoretically, multiplied until they ate every living fungi and bacteria in all of the world's oceans. In effect, it would have destroyed our entire world's ecosystem.

Conclusion of the Matter

As you can see I have taken a bit of license in my predictions. I will say that, in my opinion, everything I predicted here has some potential toward reality. Things are moving so fast in our world that the only thing we can count on is that when my son goes to bed at night, he is guaranteed to wake up in a different world.

We must hold to our faith. We cannot forget who we are and to Whom we belong.

I also believe we must resist the temptation to "check out." We cannot take the posture that the world is coming to an end every time something doubles. My wife traveled to Europe on several short-term missions' trips and on one trip she met a Christian male vocalist. His favorite saying was, "These are the last days — bread's a dollar a loaf!" Often when I talk about the doubling with people in my age-bracket or older, they reach a threshold; they roll their eyes and begin to pray, "Come, Lord Jesus." There is no easy way to say this - that is just plain quitting!

If the Lord returns before 2016, then I will be the first to shout, "Hallelujah! Beam me up, Jesus!" But this must not be our focus. We must be about the Father's business and that business is discipleship. Just last week a young man waited patiently for me after the church service. Unfortunately, I had guests coming over for lunch and therefore could not give him a long answer to his question (which was probably a good thing for him as well). He and his wife had been wondering why our church doesn't focus more on the end times. My short answer was summed up this way. First, I quoted Acts 1:6-8:

"So when they met together, they asked him, "Lord, are you at this time going to restore the kingdom to Israel?"
"He said to them: "It is not for you to know the times or dates the Father has set by his own authority. But you will receive power when the Holy Spirit comes on you; and you will be my witnesses..." (NIV)

I then added, "See that phrase, 'and you will be my witnesses...'? You see, we can't do anything about *when* the Lord returns to the earth, but we can do something about *who* will be ready when He comes."

If I have left you with more questions than answers, then so be it. I don't have that many answers myself. But this generation needs us to begin asking. Their future is too important to leave behind.

I hope this book has caused you to think about things that you may have been putting off. I hope and pray that you begin to ask the questions. Ask them of God. Ask the scriptures. Ask your pastor, friends, discipler or disciples. Talk about how we as Christians are called to respond. Ask me on my website at www.ChristianThinker.com.

I leave you with these two prayers from the Apostle Paul. These are my prayers for you.

Philippians 1:9-11 (KJV)

And this I pray, that your love may abound yet more and more in knowledge and in all judgment;
That ye may approve things that are excellent; that ye may be sincere and without offence till the day of Christ.
Being filled with the fruits of righteousness, which are by Jesus Christ, unto the glory and praise of God.

Colossians 1:9-13 (KJV)

For this cause we also, since the day we heard it, do not cease to pray for you, and to desire that ye might be filled with the knowledge of his will in all wisdom and spiritual understanding;
That ye might walk worthy of the Lord unto all pleasing, being fruitful in every good work, and increasing in the knowledge of God;
Strengthened with all might, according to his glorious power, unto all patience and longsuffering with joyfulness;
Giving thanks unto the Father, which hath made us meet to be partakers of the inheritance of the saints in light:
Who hath delivered us from the power of darkness, and hath translated us into the kingdom of his dear Son:

Epilogue:
A Tale of Two Futures

Imagine what it would have been like for our great-grandparents looking into the future and trying to see the world at 2006 from the vantage point of 1956. They could foresee some things but other aspect were unimaginable—things like the World-Wide-Web, tech support from Bangalore, India, Pocket PCs, nanotechnology, Google and cataloging the Human Genome. H.G. Wells in his attempt to see the future predicted underwater warfare, time travel and alien invasions. In 1948, George Orwell tried to see the future when he wrote *1984* and saw a technologically controlled world ruled by totalitarian governments. In 2056 I will be 97 years old. If the Lord keeps me around that long then we will see how this all turns out.

I want to conclude this book with two short stories. These are two possible worlds that could be the norm for my great-grandchildren in the year 2056. One will be an optimistic view of the world and the other, pessimistic. In each view, Jesus is still my great-grandchildren's Anchor of faith.

2056—The Enhanced Future

The v-message had just come in.

Patrick still had the occasional headache trying to adjust to his BNIE[204]upgrade. He had a few scary nights two weeks ago, when he couldn't control his dreams. Thankfully, his mom still had half a bottle of WakeGo,[205] so he was able to avoid sleep until he could get to see his Biotech.

He waited until he was in the sitting room before he took the message. Patrick relaxed with a cup of coffee. His mom had let him start drinking coffee just a year and a half ago. He still couldn't understand why she made him wait until he was fourteen to drink it; as if caffeine was a problem. She was just old-fashioned that way.

"Message three, display," Patrick commanded as he tapped his head.

The HIM[206] popped up and this time Dr. Raymond was speaking to him from behind his desk.

---

[204] BNIE – Brain Net Interface Enhancement – This device was surgically implanted in Patrick's brain just days after he was born. Patrick was the second generation to receive BNIEs at birth. Most of the initial bugs with this technology have been worked out. The first generation went through enormous trials that resulted in many deaths. It took years for people to learn to deal with the immediacy of the net. There are still people in institutions who did not learn to control the interface. Most BNIEs are still engaged with a tap on the side of the head. The thought on/off interface still causes some problems during sleep.

[205] WakeGo is a medicine that allows someone to avoid sleep for 72 hours. It stimulates the portion of the brain that regulates the need for sleep and fuels it with endorphins and dopamine.

[206] HIM – Holographic Image Messaging - Most homes have come with some type of built-in HIM system for the last 10 years. The sitting room will usually have a couch and some wonderful décor on three of the walls. The remaining wall is similar to the Wall Video Interface of the last three decades which is still found in some older homes. The HIM wall projects a 3D video image that, for all in the room, seems to be right there with them. The recent upgrade of HIM to work closely with BNIE technology has opened an entirely new art form of thought imaging.

"Hello Patrick, we reviewed your portfolio[207] and I must say, everyone in admissions is very impressed. Your paper on the worldview issues regarding the Global Cloning Ban was insightful. Your score of 98.8% is very remarkable, considering that your mom was your primary educator. Your HCOS[208] report is also very impressive. One of our admittance officials complimented your bold, Christian approach to the ethics of the debate. He suggested you might want to consider a minor in Theology to go with your Bio-ethics degree."

He paused for a moment, looked up and motioned to someone else in his office, raising a finger to indicate he was almost finished.

"Anyway, Patrick, we would love to have you join our prestigious school and company. Consider this your official acceptance message."

Patrick tapped his head and the message shut off before the obligatory logo video for Bangalore University of Biotechnology, Inc.[209] was finished.

Patrick jumped up from the couch and shouted at the top of his lungs, "MOM!!"

She was in the kitchen getting dinner ready and made sure to wipe the smile off her face before Paddy ran in. She had watched the message at the same time as Patrick through her BNIE. It was her policy to log and drop-in on any of Paddy's net communications; you cannot be too careful these days. She had suspected that this message was from the acceptance committee and couldn't keep herself from watching-in. She tried to look as stoic as possible.

---

[207] Portfolios have replaced the standard grading systems for the last 25 years. Students are judged by teams assembled by educators around the world. It became necessary to shift the focus away from standardized testing when the last traditional classrooms became obsolete in the early 30's.

[208] HCOS - Heritage Christian Online School is a Distributed Learning School that still values the parent as the primary educator.

[209] BUBtech Inc. has been the leading University/Corporation of Biotech in the world for the last fifteen years. It requires a portfolio mark of 98.23% or better for admittance.

When Patrick rushed into the kitchen, one look at his mom told him she had simulcast.

"Oh, mom, you already know," he observed with only a hint of disappointment.

They looked at each other for a whole two seconds more before they could not contain their joy any longer. Both of them burst into laughter and tears, dancing around the room. Patrick had made it to the top.

They sat down to a humble dinner. They didn't live in an extravagant home nor did they eat like the others who had his mother's net-credit level.[210] They had focused all of their credits and time on Patrick's growth, education and enhancements. Every spare credit went to ensure Patrick had the latest upgrade. Mom also felt it was necessary to teach Patrick to read from the old books, so they spent time and credits searching the antique bookstores for good classic literature. Sure, the books were available in the Google Archives[211] but she wanted him to have the sense of history that came from acquiring knowledge the way mankind had done for thousands of years. This method proved to help his exceptional development as a student. She ensured that he was well versed in the Greek Classics, which led to a proficient knowledge of that ancient world. Her masterful introduction of theology and the scriptures into his early education distinguished him as a brilliant young man in the ways

---

[210] Net-credit level – Since the great net-crash of the early 20's, all other forms of currency are abolished. Paypal undermined the entire banking system and forced the takeover of Visa and Mastercard. Their plan backfired when net-terrorists hacked Paypal and stole trillions of dollars. This thrust the world into a three-year depression that ended in war between India and the Paypal ally, The European Union. The world emerged from this with its present global economic and political structure. Corporations and countries have become much closer political allies.

[211] Google Archives – This is known as the center for all human knowledge and thought. Google finished the indexing of known print material in 2019. They almost lost everything in a surprise attack by net-terrorists during the Paypal war. The terrorists assassinated Larry Page in an effort to extract the server keys. Sergey Brin escaped and was in hiding until three year ago when he emerged and announced that Google would now begin to catalog all of mankind's thoughts by linking their BNIEs.

of the kingdom of God. He had a great Christian heritage through two of his grandparents: Dr. Christabelle Bitgood on his mother's side and Rev. Jose Fuentes on his fathers side. They were both renowned ethical Christian leaders in his ancestry who combined medicine and missions.

After dinner, Patrick wanted to go immediately to his studies but, like most other evenings, mom insisted that he go to the workout center[212] first. He made his usual run downstairs and outside to the people distributor.[213] In minutes he was working out. He hated doing this and vowed to make exercise one of his first studies in his Bioethics research at BUBtech, Inc.

When Patrick got home an hour later, he told his mom he would be in his room. She paused her conversation with her own mother and said good night. They both were so proud of Patrick. He had spent several months with his grandmother on the field in northern Uganda. Grandma Belle helped Patrick see that the world is much more than a big computer terminal. She introduced him to the needs of the less fortunate, those still in the wireless divide.[214] Pat-

---

[212] Workout center – Somewhat resembling the gyms of old, workout centers insured certain human functions such as lifting, running and swimming did not atrophy in the digital world. The genetic enhancement debate was still raging in some parts of society. *Why exercise when we can alter DNA?* Was the argument – so far the old-world bioethics were still holding on to a few non-enhancement views.

[213] The people distributor – It somewhat emulates the old-fashioned conveyors seen in airports combined with glass elevators. Because everything continues to build upward in most cities, the distributor transports people to their individual destinations as safely and efficiently as possible. In most cases all you need to do is step on the next available distributor disk and let it interface with your BNIE. With a tap and a thought you are on your way. The distributors can move people up to 100 kph throughout a big city. So far the only known deaths from distributor accidents were suicide-related when a passenger jumped out of their distributor.

[214] Wireless divide – This term refers to the parts of the world that have not been plugged in to the net because of a lack of technological human interfaces. There are two main causes for the wireless divide: countries are still operating in an old-world economy and cannot afford to provide the digital technology necessary. The company states have tried to merge but old-style politics still prevent the alliances. Secondly, there is religious resistance to

rick learned how to love while in these broken villages still ravished by old-world diseases such as malaria and AIDs. His life changed course forever when an African baby girl died in his arms from a preventable disease. *Why couldn't the corporate state solve this problem?* he thought. He prayed harder than he ever had before and dedicated himself before God to become a leader in the field of bioethics. He had sensed God's presence so deeply back there in that African village. His grandmother had prayed for him as well and asked God to use Patrick to change this horrible plight.

Both Belle and her daughter quietly cried together in the sitting room as Patrick closed his door down the hallway. Belle there in Africa and his mom in Canada knelt together and called upon their Lord for guidance over this young man's life and mind. They prayed that he would keep his sense of destiny. They both knew that God had called him to something very special.

Patrick sat on his bed, looked around and decided he would not delay any longer. He closed his eyes and with a tap on his head, focused his thoughts. *Where to begin?* His BNIE suggested a Google search; he disregarded the digital thought [215] and decided to go to the Archives himself. In two seconds, his digital self[216] was at the doors of the URL for The Google Archives. His BNIE asked what topic he would like and Patrick thought, *Bioethics, of course.* BNIE asked if

---

connecting to the global net, particularly in some Islamic regions of the world.

[215] Digital thoughts – This is the clearly distinguished inner voice of the BNIE. Early models did not differentiate between the thoughts sufficiently so that people became very confused about what their mind was speaking versus the "mind" of the net. A new personality disorder emerged known as Net Identity Syndrome.

[216] Digital self – is the term given for the virtual image of oneself as you travel the net. In the development of BNIE technology, developers transformed flat web pages into 3D websites. A person can "go" to a website now and virtually be there in their mind. The resulting picture is halfway between a vivid dream and the normal non-net world. In the latest BNIE upgrade you can view your digital self from 12 different vantage points. Most people still opt for the normal view through one's eyes.

he would please refine the search but Patrick dismissed the digital thought and proceeded through the doors.

He was in familiar territory; in fact, he loved to wander the hallways of hyperlinks[217] and lose himself in the vast stores of human knowledge. Today though, he was on a mission. Again the thought—his own this time—inquired, *Where do I start this journey in bioethics?*

Patrick was well trained in the art of net-search.[218] Mom had always taught him to start at the beginning of something. Now, if only he could figure out where the beginning was.

His thought, in command tone, pronounced, *History*. The hallway narrowed a bit but was still lengthy. *Early bioethics websites, the first 10 years,* was his next thought. This would narrow the search to something manageable. *By topic or by author,* he mused. Immediately the hallway divided in two: authors on the left side and topics on the right. Patrick wandered a ways down the hallway past the long lists of sites starting with 'A': Abortion debate, Abortion pill, Abortion rights, Abortion: Roe vs. Wade. It seemed that the list went on and on. With a bit of resignation, Patrick switched on his search assistant.[219] The hallway's lighting seemed to dim and several button-drawer links opened

---

[217] Hallways of hyperlinks – Like the ancient webpages of the last century, hyperlinks are still the way to get from one place to another on the net. In the Google Archives, the links appear as rows upon rows of buttons under various category headings, not much different from shelves and shelves of books or drawers in an ancient library.

[218] Net-search – This phrase was fast replacing the old-world word "research." Since Google had indexed all print information, research changed from a field of discovery and scholarly rigor to a skill-based discipline. It became a compulsory study just like language arts and mathematics in education. Search Bees (named after Spelling Bees) became an everyday part of children's educational experience. Patrick was a Provincial Champion Searcher-Bee when he was nine years old.

[219] Search assistant   This is a personalized virtual assistant for doing anything in the net. This net-bot is tailored to your personality and helps you to find things specific to your needs. It learns everything that can be known about you from your ancestry, education, family patterns, habits, previous searches, likes or dislikes. Recently they have been able to collect a database of your thoughts and dreams through the upgraded BNIE.

slightly with reference cards sticking out by their corners marking possible sites to visit. Patrick's time spent in the non-virtual libraries with his mom inspired him to use the classical interface[220] in the Google Archives. It made the experience feel more scholarly that way.

Patrick's search assistant opened about two dozen drawers on the right with two or three cards protruding from each drawer. He saved the links so he could read the sites over the next couple of days. Interestingly though, further down on the left side of the hallway, one drawer was open - full of entries. It was in the row marked 'B'.

Who could that be, he thought. Immediately his digital voice answered, Y*our Grandmother and...* Patrick didn't listen any further as his heart leapt at the thought of Grandma Belle's research. *Of course, she would have written about the plight in Africa. This is where I will start. After all, it was here that God called me when I was eleven, or was it twelve.* He sensed the digital voice about to answer but quickly pushed the thought out. He was eleven, actually.

As he drew closer, the button-drawers shifted position so that the "Bit-" drawer was at mid-level. The section was much larger than he had expected. There was his second cousin, Richard Jr., also his great-uncle Kenny. *Wait a minute, who is this?* This time he let his digital voice answer. *This is your great-grandfather, Gregory J Bitgood and his introductory book on the topic of a Digital World. There is a chapter, called Biotechnology, where he poses questions to the Christians in his era about the coming changes due to the exponential growth of technology.*

Normally Patrick would not linger at novelty items from the past. Maybe it was the fact that he had only known his great-grandpa while he was very young. Maybe it was this man's connection to Grandma Belle. *He was her father after all.*

---

[220] Classical Interface – Since the advent of upgrade BNIE 2.3, people have been able to customize their view of the Google Archive and other BNIE interactive sites.

I will have a look. Over the next few seconds his surroundings changed. He opened his eyes and there he was in his bedroom again. He looked over on his video wall while his BNIE interfaced with their HCI.[221] The book appeared with its bright red cover and a catchy image. The questions on the cover caught his eye: "Are you ready? Are your children ready? Do you even know what the questions are?" *Grandma Belle seemed ready. Maybe this old guy had something to say.*

He opened the book and on the fourth page, he saw it. His very own name appeared on the dedication page. Patrick quickly scrolled back a page. Greg was forty-seven when he wrote this in, *what? 2006. How could this be? What could this mean?*

He closed his eyes and instead of going to his BNIE for answers, Patrick tapped his head and turn it off.

"God, what are you saying here?"

In a still small voice, not his own, not digital, he heard within himself, "I have called you for such a time as this."

---

[221] HCI - Home Computer Interface – This technology began in the early part of the millennium in the home of the legendary Bill Gates. Computers were literally embedded into every aspect of the home and networked by the HCI. Nowadays HCIs only run the video component in the home as everything else is managed by BNIE technology.

2056 – The Deprived Future

He saw a hint of red under the smoldering wood. He had been assigned to this clean-up detail and his designated supervisor had instructed him to bring anything of value directly to him. This boss from the prison ward was temporary. Until division sent a new Enhanced[222] to tell them what to do, the prison guard would help lead the clean up. Clone 24-0000098[223] had no concept of what was valuable but he did follow orders well. Maybe he could get an extra ration of food for finding the red book.

When Clone 24-0000098 brought it to the guard, he noticed a peculiar expression on his face.

"Where did you find this?" the guard curtly demanded.

"Just over there in that pile of broken buildings," the clone answered dutifully in the usual flat, uninterested tone characteristic of all Clone responses.

The guard smiled and left saying to himself, "I can hardly wait to see what she does with this." He said it loud enough for Clone 24-0000098 to hear but it did not matter. It was all Natural human babble to him. Clones just didn't get all the nuances of what the Naturals[224] did and said.

---

[222] Enhanced is the name given to those who have had genetic enhancements in their family lines. There weren't any genetic labs in operation since the Camp wars began twenty years ago. Many of the survivors of the wars were the offspring of those who had been enhanced from 2010 to 2040. These children also carried their parents' genetic improvements. The Enhanced were in every major level of leadership in society.

[223] Clone 24-000098 – This is the 98th Clone in the 24th generation. There were thirty generations of Clones created, one for each year from 2010 to 2040. It was very unusual to see a clone with a 24 designation. They were starting to die off. Perhaps that is why this particular clone was given a simple clean-up task. There had been 9 million clones in the 24th set.

[224] Naturals were the non-enhanced humans that survived the Camp wars. There were about the same population levels of Naturals as Enhanced but numbers were declining. Some said it was evolution while others argued it was the lack of resources shared with them. Their lives were mostly spent doing grunt level work for the Corporations, some management and supervising of the Clones.

Sally Bitgood could see the light of day if she stuck her head through the bars and looked down the cellblock. Not seeing the sun was the worst part about being in prison. She didn't mind the waiting. She didn't mind the food, if you could call it that. She didn't even mind the occasional beating she would receive from the guards. Sally was a Christian and that is why she was here.[225]

Sally would pass the time praying and reading her pocket Bible. The guards had not found her precious scriptures yet. She had an old pocket New Testament that she was memorizing book by book. So far, she had memorized Ephesians, Galatians, Hebrews and 1 John. She worked hard so that she would have as much scripture inside her memory before they found the New Testament.

Not all Christians were automatically put in prison. Since the closing of the Camps,[226] only those who couldn't keep their faith to themselves ended up in prison. Sally was one of those Christians.

When Sally and her older sister had been released the first time, they were like two flowers opening up. Karen knew that in order for them to survive outside the Camps and not end up as sex slaves she had to find work for both of them. Sally wasn't worried, she had seen God's amazing

---

[225] Christians were the reason for the Camp Wars or so that is how history now reads. The Camp Wars were fought between the Global Multinational Corporation Conglomeration (GMCC) and the North American and European Union Alliance. The wars lasted for twenty years with all sides losing some power. Biotechnical weapons of mass destruction killed four out of five humans and clones on the planet. The Camps were the excuse given for fighting the wars. Christians were the scapegoats for much bigger political shifts taking over the globe. Because they were associated with the terrorist movement that destroyed the internet in 2031, Christians were the likely people to blame for the world's woes.

[226] The Camps are where most of the Christians were sent after 2031. Something had to be done with these people who believed the way they did. It seemed that they were opposed to every advancement of technology: cloning, stem cell research, computer implants. But probably the main reason they were so persecuted was that they freely spoke out against the discrimination policies of the Enhanced leaders.

answers to prayer in the past and she knew He would do it again.

The Bitgood sisters were fortunate to find a job working for a kind Enhanced family who had just lost their garden and cleaning supervisors; they had fallen in love, married and moved on. "It was all very romantic, even if they were Naturals," Mrs. Tatum would say to her friends. She would also comment on how it was a stroke of luck that she found two young girls with just the right skills to take over. She would leave out the part that they had recently been released from the Camps.

When the girls arrived, they were both introduced to their Clone workers. Both had a staff of three and both were very concerned as to how they would get along with them. The only Clones they had known up until now were the ones in the Camps. Those working the Camps were never cruel, which is actually impossible for a clone,[227] they were just indifferent. They also obeyed the guards without question.

Both Karen and Sally worked very hard but that is where their shared experienced ended. Karen was miserable; she hated working with the Clones even though they were adequate workers and got along well enough. Karen's struggle came from her memories of their father and mother. Both had died within months of each other in the Camps when Karen was only nine years old. She was put in charge of her three-year-old sister. Their parents had been

---

[227] Clones are incapable of any high level of cruelty. It is now an established fact that Clones have no moral center. The Christians would say that they are body and soul without a spirit and that God never intended humanity to live this way. They would quote James 2:26 "for the body without the spirit is dead…" This fact was first established when researchers began to study the social behavior of Eve, the very first human Clone. By the time she was sixteen, the scientists became concerned that she was not normal. She lacked any will or desire beyond what she was told. She was completely amoral. When she died in 2023 at the age of 17, scientists, psychologist and even theologians were convinced that Clones had no central sense of personhood. They had no spirit. They had no sense of good or evil and only acted out of a sense of instinct and reward. Clone behavior was never a concern.

very active in the Anti-Embryo Destruction Campaign[228] so every time Karen had to interact with Clones she felt like they had somehow taken her family away. When she would complain to her sister, Sally would simply dismiss her feelings and say, "Oh Karen, all you have to do is forgive. Mom and dad are with Jesus. They are better off there." Karen believed this but it still didn't make it any easier to forgive, especially the spiritless Clones. She would get by somehow.

Sally was exactly the opposite. She was sixteen and full of life. Sally saw her staff of three as her little flock; singing to them and sharing scriptures. She had a real breakthrough when she was able to get 28-098255 to sing with her. Eventually the whole group sang hymns and praise songs together.

Mrs. Tatum noticed something unusual about Sally. Perhaps it was how she cared for and seemed to love her three workers. She wasn't nearly as beautiful as the Enhanced girls her age and in intelligence the difference was as pronounced as a kindergarten student next to a college graduate. Sally was a Natural but there was a recognizable quality about her. Mrs. Tatum had never met a girl like Sally before and she knew it was her faith that made Sally so special. Mrs. Tatum had been dealing with a sense of doom for years. Her son died in a drowning accident and neither she nor her husband had dealt well with it. One evening Sally and her staff were cleaning up after a dinner party of Enhanced delegates.

"Tell me what you think about heaven, Sally?" she asked.

---

[228] The Anti-Embryo Destruction Campaign was the global movement against the selection process for finding suitable persons to clone. The process involved testing their stem cells through fertilizing multiple embryos before they attempted to clone them. This resulted in literally billions of embryos created and needlessly killed. The right to life movement took a stand that nearly every other religious and social group did not understand.

Sally didn't realize that she was about to cross a threshold making her a criminal.[229] She began to share about heaven and hell. She spoke of the forgiveness of Jesus and the love of God. She shared the Gospel with this beautiful, intelligent woman with such simplicity that it profoundly affected Mrs. Tatum. She invited Jesus into her heart and life that evening.

When Mr. Tatum walked in on the two of them praying, he was stunned. Without a single moment of hesitation, he reached for the radiophone and called the Corporation Enforcement Team. By the morning of the next day, Sally and Karen were carted off to prison.

Sally and Karen were sent to different wings and rarely saw each other. Prisoners were released from their cells for one hour each day but the girls were on different schedules. Because they had so ill effected an Enhanced, they were considered as bad as terrorists[230] and several of the guards called them so. This did not fare well with the other women in the prison so they were forced to stay by themselves most of the time.

One guard in particular seemed to despise Sally. Apparently, his family had been selected to enter the ge-

---

[229] One of the conditions of closing the Camps was that Christians would not be allowed to recruit other followers. Proselytizing was considered a major offence and would result in years in prison.

[230] A Christian "fundamentalist" group known as the Anti-Embryo Destruction League for Christ (AEDLC) were responsible for Christians all over the world being identified as terrorists. They had caused several minor problems in AjBiotech – the company responsible for the policy that resulted in the massive destruction of human embryos, bombing their labs and threatening their executives. The world responded by getting behind AjBiotech and supporting their position. The AEDLC felt that they had no choice but to "hold the world responsible." They launched a series of attacks on the net. They were able to successfully load a self-replicating virus in the Google Archives. Within two weeks, the world's information was mush. Next, they sent the same virus into the world banking system at Paypal Corp. Finally they unleashed an army of nano-bots that ate away the lining on the fiber optics that carried the backbone of the net. These three attacks, in the fall of 2031, brought the world to its knees and completely destroyed the internet. In the next two years, Christians everywhere were being sent to the Camps.

netic enhancement program just before the net crashed.[231] He was born eleven months later and blamed the Christians that he was a Natural.

He would get back a piece of his pain that day. He had the book in his possession and planned to taunt the young girl with it.

Sally was awakened from a nap to behold the guard laughing on the other side of the bars. He had a faded red book in his hand but she couldn't make out the title. She cleared her eyes and read the word "Digital." The rest of the cover was too hard to read.

The guard threw it down before her cell and spit on it. With seething hate in every word, he said, "Just as your family has ruined my life so will I to any memory of yours."

Sally had no idea what he was talking about. She tried to swallow back the fear and replied, "I don't know why you hate me so much but I know that with God's help you can forgive."

He unzipped his pants and said, "This is what I think of your God and His help and this is what I do to you and your father or whoever this is." He proceeded to urinate on the book. When he was done, he kicked it into the cell, told her to lick it all off and walked away.

When he left she laid there shaking and in shock. She was sure he had intended to rape her that day. Thankfully, God had protected her. The pungent smell of his urine filled her cell and she remembered the book. Did the guard realize that he had broken multiple protocols by leaving a book in her cell? She leaned over her bed to get a better look and could not believe her eyes. The title read something about a Digital World but the author's name stood out clearly - Greg Bitgood. *Who was Greg Bitgood?* She forced

---

[231] When the net crashed in 2031 nearly all research, scientific activity and genetic enhancement ceased. Without the Google Archives, most of the scientists were simply lost in the laboratories. The fiber optics had been eaten away and there really wasn't the economic and manufacturing ability to replace the trillions of miles of wire. Sure, there was still wireless technology but it had no backbone to build on.

herself to pick up the wet book and opening to the first few pages she read,

> "I dedicate this book to my great-grandchildren, Patrick Fuentes and Sally Bitgood, who will either be in cyber-university when they access the audible version of this book found in the Google Archives, or in jail when a sadistic guard notices the last name of the author and throws a copy of the book that was found in the smoldering ruins of the Christian Camps."

God in his providence had used a bitter prison guard to send her a prophetic message of love. God had known all along that Sally would be here one day and need to hear His voice of love.

Postscript to These Stories

I realize that I have used every bit of literary license available to tell these two stories. My goal was not to glorify my family's place in history. My goal was to help us all think about two possible, and I would say, plausible futures.

My obvious hope is to continue to ride the doubling to the Enhanced Future, but at what cost? Should we not take issue with this brave new world? At what point do we lose our humanity in the melding of machines. Obviously, the church was successful in maintaining its identity and acceptance in Patrick's future. But are Christians able to stand out and truly influence a world like this or do we get lulled to sleep as we have so many times throughout the Church's history.

The darker world of Sally Bitgood, in my opinion has a much greater probability than Patrick's future. If the doubling continues, eventually something has to give. The voice of a few radical Christians can be heard loud and clear in the Digital World. I marvel how in our day a small group of several thousand terrorists can bring the planet o i s knees. How much more after ten more doublings?

There are a few things that both stories have in common that I consider to be unavoidable in the next 50 years, should Jesus tarry. Both futures had massive shifts in global politics caused by the change of power to multinational companies. Doubling of the mandate, size and wealth of companies like Microsoft, Intel and Google invaded every area of their lives. They wanted more and more power as time moved on. Their global ability to move to any place that would facilitate their goals only meant there was no government that would be able to limit them. In both futures the biotechnologies were still the reason for social debate. These technologies will, without a doubt, create the most challenging ethical debates in human history. We must get ready for the enormous weight this will place on the church, our culture, our governments, our schools and ultimately, our children. Finally, both futures still saw vibrant Christian experience. Jesus will be very much alive and with us in 2056 or should I say with our great-grandchildren. The work of discipleship will continue and the Kingdom of God will not be stopped by any technology, multinational or genetic enhancement. God knew all this was coming when, in His sovereignty, He created a Digital World. Jesus could not have said it any plainer:

Matthew 16:18

...This is the rock on which I will put together my church, a church so expansive with energy that not even the gates of hell will be able to keep it out.

(The Message)

I pray Godspeed to you and your children.

Index

1 Corinthians 9.19-23, 47, 53
1 Peter 2.11, 22, 51
1 Peter 3.15, 40
2 Peter 3.13, 28

A

Abortion, 150, 195
AdWords, 125
Al Qaeda, 107
Aliens, 7, 50
Amish, 7, 48, 49, 50, 52

B

Babel, 96, 99, 100, 101, 102, 103,
    104, 117
Bangalore, India, 107, 141, 181,
    189, 191
Barksdale, Jim, 81, 82
Barna Group, 108, 109, 178
Berners-Lee, Tim, 80
Bioethics, 144, 145, 149, 150, 155,
    156, 157, 162, 163, 191, 193, 195
Biomolecular Nanotechnology,
    176
Bitgood, Ken, 110, 111, 112, 132
Blog, 84, 85, 92, 93, 132
Blogs, 85
Blue Gene, 174
Bodanis, David, 28, 29
Borg, 162
Brain-Machine Interfaces, 160
Brin, Sergey, 119, 120, 121, 122,
    123, 124, 125, 126, 127, 130,
    136, 183, 192
Bush, George, 81, 85, 153

C

Center For Bioethics and
    Human Dignity, 144
Cheshire, Dr. William, 157

Christian Schools, 183
Cloning, 23, 154, 155, 156, 157, 158,
    164, 182, 185, 198, 199, 200, 201
Cochlear implants, 160
Codex, 68, 91
Collins, Dr. Francis, 144
Content filter, 89
Creator, 20, 51, 138, 142, 143
Cyborg, 162

D

Deep Blue, 174
Department of Defense, 50, 79, 181
Designer Babies, 149, 150
Digital Bible Society, 111, 115,
    132
Disciples, 8, 86
Discipleship, 7, 41, 43, 52, 54, 55,
    58, 60, 89, 117
Discipling, 2, 3, 4
Dispensationalism, 116
DNA, 29, 140, 143, 144, 148, 151,
    152, 154, 155, 163, 176, 177,
    180, 181, 183, 193
Dolly the Sheep, 8, 154, 155, 156
Double, 9, 177
Doubling, 9, 169, 170, 171, 174,
    177, 205

E

Ebay, 83
ego-search, 128
Einstein, Albert, 28, 167
Electricity, 29
Embryo, 146, 148, 149, 150, 152,
    153, 156
embryo adoption, 152
Enhancing, 8, 39, 141, 145, 146,
    159, 174, 177
Ethnos, 52, 53, 56
Evangelical, 16, 18, 86, 108

Exodus 20.3-5, 38
exponential curve, 32, 172, 173

F

Frankenstein, 137, 138, 139
Friedman, Thomas, 63, 81, 104, 105, 106
Friedrich the Wise, 77

G

Galatians 5.14, 52, 56
Garreau, Joel, 39, 141, 146, 159, 173, 174, 177
Gates, Bill, 18, 120, 126, 185, 197
Genesis 1.3, 27
Genesis 2.17, 21
genetic engineering, 145, 146, 164
Germ-line genetics, 146
Global, 8, 109, 112, 113, 183, 185, 191, 199
Globalization, 8, 9, 23, 94, 104, 105, 106, 107, 132, 181
Google, 5, 8, 18, 89, 119, 121, 122, 123, 124, 125, 126, 127, 128, 129, 130, 131, 132, 133, 134, 135, 136, 161, 181, 182, 183, 189, 192, 194, 195, 196, 202, 203, 204, 205
Gore, Al, 81
Great Commission, 42, 48, 49, 52, 54, 57
Great Firewall of China, 115, 131
Gutenberg, 8, 23, 71, 72, 73, 74, 78, 126

H

Hayden, Pat, 88
HCOS, 11, 191
Hebrews 1.3, 28
Henry, Joseph, 29, 30, 31, 126, 172
Heritage Christian Online School, 13, 16, 86, 88, 191
Heritage Christian School, 12, 87, 88, 137, 139

Hewitt, Hugh, 84, 85, 92
HTTP, 80, 81, 82
Human Genome Project., 143, 145

I

Informationalism, 8, 9, 23, 119, 127, 135, 183
Intel, 38, 126, 171, 172, 173, 177, 182, 183, 205
Intelligent Design, 142

J

Jetsons, 82
John 17.11, 21
John 8.31-32, 60
Jude 3, 55

K

Kalamen, Bodie, 11, 13, 41
Kasparov, Gary, 174
Keaggy, Phil, 57
Kelowna Christian Center, 12, 14, 41
Kilner, John, 155, 156, 162, 163
Knorr, Dan, 85, 107
Knowledge, 8, 132
Kosovo, 114

L

Luther, Martin, 8, 71, 73, 74, 75, 76, 77, 91, 92, 93

M

Matthew 22
   38-40, 56
Matthew 28
   18-20, 42, 43, 52, 53, 55
McLuhan, Marshall, 37
Microsoft, 126, 127, 131, 173, 183, 205
Moore, Gordon, 38, 172, 177
Morse, Henry, 31, 126
Motilone, 43, 44, 45, 46, 47, 53
MSN, 83, 90

N

Nanotechnology, 9, 39, 175, 176
Nathanson, Dr. Bernard, 150,
    151
National Nanotechnology
    Initiative, 175, 177
nationalism, 55, 117
Netscape, 81, 82
Nimrod, 96, 97, 98, 99, 100, 101,
    103, 104
Noah, 96, 97, 98, 99, 100, 101, 103

O

Olson, Bruce, 43, 44, 45, 46, 47, 52,
    53

P

Page, Larry, 81, 82, 103, 105, 109,
    119, 120, 121, 122, 123, 124,
    125, 126, 127, 130, 137, 141,
    174, 176, 178, 192
Postman, Neil, 20, 36, 37, 67, 134
pro-life, 150, 151, 154, 181

R

Reformation, 8, 23, 71, 73, 74, 76
Renaissance, 73
Reproductive cloning, 156
Robots, 159, 160, 162

S

Schmidt, Eric, 125
Shelley, Mary, 137, 138, 139
Sherley, James, 154
Skype, 83

Socrates, 8, 65, 66, 67
Somatic gene engineering, 146
Star Trek, 103, 141, 161
Stem Cell, 8, 151, 153
super mice, 147

T

TCP/IP, 79, 80, 82
Technorati, 84, 85, 129
Telegraph, 32
Thamus, 65, 66, 67, 73
the image of God, 150, 158, 162,
    163, 164
therapeutic cloning, 156
Theuth, 65, 66, 73
Tower of Babel, 96
Transistor, 34
Transistors, 34, 35
Tyndale, William, 77

U

Ubiquity, 7, 35
Uganda, 113, 183, 193
URL, 83, 194

W

Warren, Rick, 169
wet labs, 140
Wisdom, 133
WWJD, 19
www.ym4c.ca, 88
Wycliffe, John, 69, 70, 71

Y

Y2K, 18
Yahoo, 123, 127
Young Minds for Canada, 88